D1515988

PRESENTED AS A SERVICE TO MEDICINE BY MERCK SHARP & DOHME

AMITRIPTYLINE IN THE MANAGEMENT OF DEPRESSION

PUBLISHED BY MERCK SHARP & DOHME
DIVISION OF MERCK & CO., INC., WEST POINT, PA. 19486
1975

ISBN NUMBER
911910-74-3

LIBRARY OF CONGRESS
CATALOG CARD
NUMBER 74-290-65

PRINTED IN THE
UNITED STATES
OF AMERICA

PUBLISHER'S NOTE

In the following chapters, recognized authorities in the field of depression draw from their vast clinical experience to present a definitive analysis of the clinical application of a highly effective tricyclic antidepressant—amitriptyline.

Beginning with a historical perspective of the treatment of depression and the breakthrough represented by the advent of tricyclic antidepressants, the authors discuss the usefulness of amitriptyline in numerous types of depressed patients treated in a variety of clinical settings. Within this framework is also presented an up-to-date evaluation of many of the epidemiological, social, and economic factors involved in depression, which illustrate the high incidence of the disease in modern society and the critical need to diagnose and treat it effectively.

One overriding theme that colors the entire presentation is that any medication, including amitriptyline, is only as effective as the involvement on the part of the physician administering it. The point is clearly made, for example, that many depressions can be successfully treated by the primary physician through brief counseling sessions and adequate antidepressant therapy without referring the patient for psychiatric care. Other more difficult cases requiring psychiatric referral, however, are also discussed. Moreover, the rewards of successful management of depression are shown to be as great for the physician as they are for the patient.

It is not intended, however, that the chapters presented in this text be the sole source of prescribing information for amitriptyline or any other product mentioned by the authors. The current Direction Circular must be regarded as the appropriate source of prescribing information, and the reader should consult it before prescribing or administering any product. Specifically, for amitriptyline and any other products mentioned that are available from Merck Sharp & Dohme, current Direction Circulars, including contraindications, warnings, precautions, and adverse reactions, have been included in the back of this book.

I

AMITRIPTYLINE IN THE MANAGEMENT OF DEPRESSION

PRESENTED AS A SERVICE TO MEDICINE
BY MERCK SHARP & DOHME

CONTRIBUTING AUTHORS

JUDD MARMOR, M.D.
Franz Alexander Professor of Psychiatry
University of Southern California
School of Medicine
Los Angeles, California

JAMES MAAS, M.D.
Professor of Psychiatry
Yale University
School of Medicine
New Haven, Connecticut

ERNEST HARTMANN, M.D.
Director, Sleep and Dream Laboratory
Boston State Hospital
Boston, Massachusetts

JOHN J. SCHWAB, M.D.
Professor of Psychiatry and Medicine
University of Louisville
School of Medicine
Louisville, Kentucky

ALVIN I. GOLDFARB, M.D.
Associate Clinical Professor of Psychiatry
The Mount Sinai School of Medicine
The City University of New York
New York, New York

GERALD L. KLERMAN, M.D.
Professor of Psychiatry
Harvard Medical School
Boston, Massachusetts

A.L. NELSON BLODGETT, M.D.
Assistant Professor of Psychiatry
U.C.L.A. School of Medicine
Los Angeles, California

ALLEN J. ENELOW, M.D.
Chairman, Department of Psychological
and Social Medicine
Presbyterian Hospital of Pacific
Medical Center
San Francisco, California

TABLE OF CONTENTS

AMITRIPTYLINE IN THE MANAGEMENT OF DEPRESSION

COMPREHENSIVE MANAGEMENT OF DEPRESSION: HISTORICAL PERSPECTIVE AND CURRENT CONCEPTS

JUDD MARMOR, M.D.
Franz Alexander Professor of Psychiatry
University of Southern California
School of Medicine
Los Angeles, California

Judd Marmor, M.D. is the Franz Alexander Professor of Psychiatry at University of Southern California School of Medicine, President-Elect (1974-75) of the American Psychiatric Association, and President of the Group for the Advancement of Psychiatry. He is a past president of the American Academy of Psychoanalysis and of the Southern California Psychoanalytic Society and Institute, and a Fellow of the American College of Psychiatrists.

Dr. Marmor is also on the Editorial Board of *The American Journal of Psychoanalysis, Contemporary Psychoanalysis, Comprehensive Psychiatry, The Archives of Sexual Behavior,* and *The American Journal of Community Psychology.* He is the author of over 180 technical articles dealing with several subjects in psychiatry, and a selection of these papers has been published as a book. He is the recipient of numerous awards for his distinguished contributions.

COMPREHENSIVE MANAGEMENT OF DEPRESSION: HISTORICAL PERSPECTIVE AND CURRENT CONCEPTS

INTRODUCTION

Historical Perspective

In a curious kind of way psychiatry seems to have come around almost a full circle in its conceptualization of the depressive disorders. Physicians in the nineteenth century were strongly convinced that these disorders were the consequences of some inherent biological "defect" of genetic origin. In the course of the first half of the twentieth century, however, largely under the influence of psychoanalysis, most psychiatrists tended to move away from the biological defect theory toward an emphasis that was mainly psychodynamic. Within the context of the latter framework, depressive disorders were conceived of as reactions to a serious object loss, actual or symbolic, or to frustrated hostility "turned backward on the self." Now we have returned, albeit with considerably more sophistication, to a belief that notwithstanding the existence of such psychodynamic elements there are indeed relevant genetic and biochemical factors in many depressive reactions that cannot be ignored.

The patterns of antidepressant therapy have paralleled the shifting concepts of these disorders. From the relatively crude physical interventions of the nineteenth century, the emphasis gradually shifted to the essentially psychotherapeutic approaches of the 1930s and 40s. These approaches had a reasonable modicum of success, particularly with the so-called neurotic or reactive depressions that had been triggered by an obvious traumatic stress, or in which an underlying neurotic personality disorder was playing a major role in the depressive reaction. But the results of psychotherapy with the more serious psychotic depressions were much less satisfactory.

Chemical Therapy

Consequently there were continued efforts to find ways of augmenting or enhancing the effects of psychotherapy through the adjuvant use of drugs that might help to modify the patient's mood. Among the earliest that gained wide usage were the amphetamines, which seemed at times to be helpful in lifting the spirits of mildly depressed individuals. Basically, however, the amphetamines functioned as stimulants rather than as genuine antidepressants, and they proved to be of little sustained value in the treatment of more serious depressions. Moreover, their stimulating effect was often followed by a depressive rebound that could be very distressing.

The search for more effective techniques then led to the introduction of various forms of "shock" therapy. In the early 1930s Sakel introduced insulin coma therapy for the treatment of schizophrenia, but it was found to have no value in the treatment of depressive disorders. Shortly afterwards, von Meduna introduced convulsive therapy by Metrazol (pentamethylenetetrazol) injection. There was a 30-second lag between the time of injection of the drug and the onset of convulsions, however, during which patients often experienced either acute discomfort or sheer panic. The result was that they dreaded this therapy and often had to be literally dragged protestingly to the "Metrazol room"—a most unpleasant experience for everyone concerned.

Electroshock Therapy

Fortunately, around the same time Cerletti and Bini discovered electric convulsive treatment, which proved to be not only simpler but also more reliable than Metrazol therapy and soon displaced it entirely. Electroshock therapy has continued to be an extremely useful technique for the handling not only of the severe depressive disorders but also of some acute schizophrenic reactions. It suffers, however, from a number of disadvantages, philosophically as well as clinically. Philosophically, it is first of all a purely pragmatic technique, the *modus operandi* of which has never been clearly understood. Secondly, it is an approach that goes counter to the basic humanistic foundations of psychiatric thought. Many psychiatrists find it difficult to do violence to other human beings even though the motivation is therapeutic. The well-known quip that "a psychiatrist is a physician who can't stand the sight of blood" is a reflection of this state of mind. Clinically, the potential complications of ECT are not to be taken lightly. The possibility of vertebral or other fractures exists even though newer techniques of ECT administration, utilizing prior injection of muscle relaxants, have reduced these to a minimum. There is also concern about precipitating a vascular episode, particularly in patients with existing cardiovascular disease. Finally, the fact that some impairment of memory, however transient, almost always occurs is also a drawback. Indeed, when ECT was improperly given too often and over too long a time, as it sometimes was in its early days, the equivalent of an "electrical lobotomy" was the end result.

Thus, despite the fact that ECT could produce a remission more rapidly than any other technique and was demonstrably an effective technique for the treatment of psychotic depression, many psychiatrists employed it with caution, and often only as a last resort, after other therapeutic approaches had been given an adequate trial. It is not surprising, therefore, that when the antidepressant drugs were discovered in the late 1950s and were found to be therapeutically effective, they were welcomed with open arms by the large majority of psychiatrists.

ANTIDEPRESSANT CHEMOTHERAPY

Theoretical Considerations

Happiness and sadness are not just states of mind; they are also specific neurochemical states, as are all emotions. Contemporary concepts concerning the neurochemistry of depression began in 1951 with the discovery that when iproniazid was used for the chemotherapy of tuberculosis it produced a state of increased energy and elevation of mood. This led to its successful utilization in the treatment of depressive states. Subsequent research demonstrating that iproniazid is a monoamine oxidase inhibitor, and that the monoamine oxidase enzyme plays an important role in the metabolism of brain amines, focused attention on the role of the amines in depression. Animal studies demonstrated that MAO inhibitors increase the brain levels of serotonin and norepinephrine, an increase that led to a heightening both of mood and of motor activity. Thus the hypothesis evolved that depression might be related to a decrease or functional unavailability of amines in the central nervous system.

This hypothesis was fortified by the subsequent discovery in 1957 that imipramine and, subsequently, amitriptyline, both tricyclic compounds, were equally or more effective in the treatment of depression than the MAO inhibitors although they acted in a different way. Their action was to decrease cell permeability to norepinephrine, thus increasing its available concentration at the synapses.

In contrast to the amphetamines which are euphoriants and stimulants, the MAO inhibitors and tricyclic compounds like imipramine and amitriptyline are antidepressants rather than euphoriants or stimulants. Thus they have little euphoriant action on normals despite their marked antidepressant effect in patients with depressive disorders.

The MAO Inhibitors

The MAO inhibitors were the first major antidepressant agents to be utilized and were often dramatic in their effects. It soon became evident, however, that they had some disturbing, and sometimes dangerous, side effects. All of them tended to potentiate any ingested pressor substances, leading to hypertensive crises with severe headache, nausea, and vomiting. Foods containing appreciable amounts of tyramine, such as well-ripened soft cheeses, were particularly apt to trigger such crises in patients taking MAO inhibiting drugs. Indeed, the number of substances that might trigger attacks is fairly substantial, and includes such other substances as liquor, beer, wine, yogurt, amphetamine, nasal sprays or any other drugs containing sympathomimetic agents, etc. In the light of such hazards, many psychiatrists stopped using the MAO inhibitors in outpatient practice and restricted their use to inpatient settings, since an individual in an outpatient setting might unwittingly be exposed to some triggering substance and be subjected to a highly unpleasant if not dangerous experience. In a controlled institutional setting, of course, the risks are considerably lower.

The Tricyclics

Because they were free from these dangerous side effects and yet were equally effective therapeutically, the tricyclic antidepressants quickly won favor in clinical practice. Imipramine was the first to be introduced and was a very satisfactory agent except for the fact that there was often a fairly prolonged delay of three weeks or more before its therapeutic effects began to be manifest. When amitriptyline became available, it likewise achieved popularity, despite a similar delay in antidepressant effect.

The search for the "ideal" antidepressant continues, however. When and if it is found, it will probably need to be taken only once a day, will manifest its specific therapeutic effect within hours or days rather than in weeks, and will be essentially nontoxic with no significant side effects. Meanwhile, however, the clinician can be gratified that the present group of tricyclic antidepressants are reasonably safe and effective.

THE FAMILY PHYSICIAN
AND THE COMPREHENSIVE
TREATMENT OF DEPRESSION

The large majority of depressed patients with the exception of the severely psychotic or acutely suicidal ones can and should be treated by the family physician. He represents the first "line of defense" in the treatment of mental and emotional disorders. He is often the first professional to see these patients, and the one who has the opportunity therefore to intervene in the disorder in its early stages.

The Need for Involvement

But to function most effectively, he must be willing and able to involve himself with the patient in a significant way. I am fully aware of the inordinate pressures of time under which the usual family practitioner operates. However, it may take far less time than he thinks to be helpful to such patients. Fifteen minutes of focused interviews with the patient two or three times a week can elicit a great deal of relevant material and enable the physician to gain an understanding of the multiple factors that may be contributing to his patient's disorder and to deal with them meaningfully. His willingness to take this time and his human concern and empathy will strongly reinforce the effect of any antidepressant medication he prescribes.

Chemotherapy

As part of such a comprehensive approach, the tricyclic antidepressants will often be found to be particularly useful. The mere prescribing of almost any medication under such circumstances tends to have some placebo effect, but it has been demonstrated in numerous double-blind studies that the tricyclic antidepressants have a specific therapeutic effect that clearly exceeds any nonspecific placebo action.

The Effect of Environment

Ideally, the physician confronted with any disorder should endeavor—as effectively as he can—to neutralize all of the pathogenic factors contributing to that disorder. Even in patients with strong genetic predispositions to depression, we are always dealing with an interplay of factors, some of which are intrinsic to the individual, others of which reflect external factors. In an absolute sense biological, psychodynamic, and sociocultural factors are all involved in the final common denominator that we call behavior, whether it be normal or pathological.

For example, we may postulate that in persons with endogenous depressions there may be an innate abnormality in certain neuro-regulatory mechanisms that predisposes such individuals to repeated severe depressive reactions. But even so, these reactions do not occur capriciously and for no reason at all. To assume that would go counter to everything we know about psychophysiologic causality. What the presumptive genetic "defect" means is that such individuals are biologically prone to respond pathologically to stresses, perhaps even to relatively minor stresses, much more easily than do "normal" individuals.

In dealing with such patients therapeutically, therefore, even though some therapists may choose to place the major emphasis on correcting or compensating for the apparent neurochemical defect, it does not mean that they are justified in ignoring the stressful factors that may be present in the patient's interpersonal or sociocultural life situation. Indeed, to do so may tend to vitiate the therapeutic effect of the antidepressant agent. On the other hand, concomitantly treating the relevant psychodynamic factors serves to reinforce the beneficial effect of the drug.

Typical Case

Consider, for example, the following not uncommon clinical case. A middle-aged housewife with a history of several previous depressive episodes and a positive family history for depression breaks down during the menopausal period with a severe depressive reaction of psychotic proportions, weeps frequently, sleeps poorly, has no appetite, and has no desire to do anything. She talks of wishing she were dead, feels worthless, describes herself as an "empty shell." In the course of our interview with her we sense strong feelings of anger on her part toward her husband and her only son, even though these feelings are usually followed by expressions of self-reproach. The background history reveals that the patient was a somewhat compulsive individual who had lived entirely for her husband, her child, and her home. She had very few friends outside of her immediate family and had no outside interests. In recent years her husband had become less attentive, and their sex life had deteriorated. Concurrently, she had begun to express concern about losing her looks and getting "old," and also about changes in her menstrual patterns indicating that she was going through the "change of life." Her severe depressive reaction developed several weeks following the marriage of her only son and his moving into his own apartment.

Here we have a woman with an apparent genetic tendency toward depression and a history of several previous episodes, now presenting with another one in the involutional period of her life. The severity of her depression makes any exclusively psychotherapeutic approach impractical. Although she might once have been considered an excellent candidate for electro-shock therapy, our tendency today would be to put her on a tricyclic antidepressant and increase it to effective dosages as rapidly as possible. But almost all psychiatrists would agree that to do *only* that would not be doing justice to the patient. Even if she responded favorably to the medication, the odds under such circumstances would be very great that before long she would come through the "revolving door" with a recurrence, because nothing would have been done to modify what had become for her an intolerable life situation.

In addition to receiving medication, therefore, such a patient needs to feel, first, that the doctor regards her with concern and is genuinely interested in helping her. This is of paramount corrective emotional importance to a patient who is feeling worthless and unneeded. Second, efforts must be made to help her husband and son understand and respond constructively to her emotional needs. And third, as our medication renders her more amenable to psychotherapy, every effort must be made to help the patient herself understand how and why she has so unwisely narrowed the base of her emotional security and to assist her in broadening her life interests and increasing her self-esteem. In these ways we endeavor to comprehensively modify the total "system" of her life—biologically, psychodynamically, and interpersonally—and so to minimize the likelihood that another depressive reaction will occur.

Differentiation in Diagnosis

The question of whether neurotic and psychotic depressions are two completely distinct disorders or merely represent opposite ends of a quantitative and qualitative continuum, with a borderland area in which the two cannot be clearly differentiated, is still a disputed and unresolved issue in psychiatry. One way of looking at this problem, however, is to weigh the relative importance of endogenous and exogenous factors in the balance of forces that have led to the psychological decompensation. When we see patients with frequent recurrent depressive reactions developing in the absence of any outstanding life stresses and with a positive family history for depression, we are justified in suspecting a strong endogenous basis for the depressions and to pay primary attention to correcting the presumptive underlying neurochemical disorder. On the other hand, when depressive reactions develop in response to a significant traumatic life situation or object loss in individuals with a negative family history, we are more likely to think in terms of a neurotic or reactive depression, particularly if the symptoms are not of psychotic proportions. In such situations we may tend to play down the neurochemical approach, and place our major emphasis on modifying the stressful life situation and psychotherapeutically supporting the patient's ego and increasing his or her coping capacity. In still other instances, indeed in most, we may see an interplay of endogenous and exogenous factors that require that we pay equal attention to both. In *all* instances, however, the *whole* patient and the *whole* life situation must be taken into consideration for optimal therapeutic results.

We can give a patient agents that keep him awake, put him to sleep, energize him, agitate him, slow him down, or speed him up. But no drug in and of itself can be a total substitute for enabling a patient to cope with his life situation more effectively. Drugs can be and are a tremendous help to us in these efforts, but they are not a substitute for the human element. People still need people, and the disturbed patient needs that touch of humanity that an interested and empathic physician offers. This is at the heart of all psychotherapy, whether it be dynamic psychotherapy, group therapy, or just sitting down and listening to a patient's troubles. The fact that there *is* someone who is interested and concerned is a vital element in the total therapeutic approach to depression. The primary physician who first sees the depressed patient has a unique opportunity to provide this element even as he supplements it with any indicated medication. It is an element of paramount importance in the treatment of the depressed patient—the foundation stone upon which the structure of all other therapeutic interventions rests.

THEORIES OF MODES AND SITES OF ACTION

JAMES MAAS, M.D.
Professor of Psychiatry
Yale University
School of Medicine
New Haven, Connecticut

James Maas, M.D. is Professor of Psychiatry at Yale University School of Medicine and Chairman of the National Institute of Mental Health Collaborative Study on the Psychobiology of Depressive Illnesses. He is a member of the Editorial Board of both *Psychosomatic Medicine* and *Psychopharmacological Communications*.

Dr. Maas is a Fellow of Davenport College, Yale University and is a Diplomate and Fellow of the American Board of Psychiatry. Included among his many professional affiliations are Charter Membership, Steering Committee, The Society for Neuroscience, and Fellowship in the American Psychiatric Association. He has received many awards and honors for teaching and research and has published many technical papers dealing with the pharmacology and biochemistry of psychiatric disturbances.

THEORIES OF MODES AND SITES OF ACTION

PREFACE

The mechanism(s) of action of tricyclic antidepressants in man is not known. This chapter, therefore, will primarily concern itself with the modes of action of amitriptyline and other similar drugs on biogenic amine disposition in the central nervous system of mammalian species other than man. Initial comments will be directed toward structure-activity relationships. These will be followed by a representative and, hopefully, synthetic review of the available data as to the ways in which amitriptyline and other drugs of this type alter the disposition and the turnover of DA, 5-HT, and NE. Finally, studies dealing with the effects of these drugs in man will be reviewed.

BACKGROUND

Two Significant Observations

In the 1950s, two series of accidental observations were made which were to have important consequences for both the treatment and the understanding of the genesis of the affective disorders:

1. A small but significant number of patients being treated for hypertension with the rauwolfia alkaloids developed severe depressions which were indistinguishable from naturally occurring depressive disorders.

2. Patients being treated for tuberculosis with iproniazid had elevations in mood which seemed to be above and beyond those which would be expected from the improvement in their physical health.

Drugs and the Role of Biogenic Amines in Regulating Mood

Effects of reserpine and iproniazid: The general concept that the biogenic amines dopamine (DA), serotonin (5-HT), and norepinephrine (NE) had an important role in regulating mood states began to emerge when pharmacological investigations indicated that reserpine (a rauwolfia alkaloid) produced a depletion of these amines in brain and other tissues, whereas iproniazid produced an elevation of these amines via monoamine oxidase inhibition. (For reviews, see references 1, 2, 3.)

Effects of the tricyclic antidepressants: In the early days of these investigations, an important inconsistency in these amine hypotheses of the affective disorders was noted: namely, that the tricyclic antidepressants, of which amitriptyline is an example, were effective in the treatment of severe depressive states but did not produce significant changes in amine levels in the brain. Subsequently, it was discovered[4] that these agents were capable of blocking the reuptake of biogenic amines—the principal mechanism of inactivation of these putative neurotransmitters—and so the amine hypotheses of the affective disorders assumed greater currency.

Since these earlier observations, there has been much basic and clinical pharmacological research aimed at understanding the specific modes of action of the tricyclic antidepressants with the hope being that such an improved understanding might help us to better understand the nature of the biological disorder which results in mania or depression. It is also anticipated that such information will assist in the choice of a particular antidepressant for a particular patient.

GENERAL STRUCTURE-ACTIVITY RELATIONSHIPS

The structures of amitriptyline and imipramine are given in Figure 1 to add greater appreciation and perspective regarding structure-activity relationships and data on modes of action of amitriptyline, its demethylated product, and other tricyclic

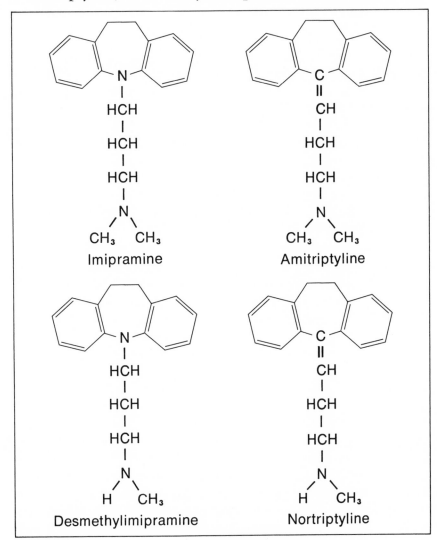

Fig. 1. Tricyclic Antidepressants

19

antidepressants. In addition, their demethylated products (nor-triptyline and desmethylimipramine) are shown for purposes of clarity, since these conversions occur *in vivo* and are important in terms of the drugs' actions.

Spatial Arrangement and Substitution

Bickell and Brodie[5] approached the problem of the structure-activity relationships by using an animal behavior model; when animals were treated with a benzoquinolazine, they developed a sedated, reserpine-like syndrome and in varying degrees this behavioral state could be blocked or prevented by a number of analogs of tricyclic antidepressants. In brief, they noted that activity was restricted to compounds having two or three carbons on the side chain. Compounds with branch chains or chains containing more than four carbons tended to be either inactive or toxic. In terms of N substitution, activity was confined to methyl substituted or unsubstituted amines, whereas ethyl or higher alkyl groups on the side chain nitrogen resulted in compounds which were either inactive or toxic. A number of ring substituted compounds were active, i.e., the 3-chloro, 10-methyl, or the 10, 11-dimethyl. Changes in the bridge between the two phenyl groups from $-CH_2-CH_2-$ to $-CH=CH-$ did not change activity. Removal of the ring nitrogen and substitution with a carbon had little effect on activity.

Molecular Configuration and Therapeutic Effect

Another group of investigators[6,7,8,9] examined structure-activity relationships via more direct biochemical measurements, i.e., blockage of the uptake of norepinephrine by rabbit aortic strips or brain. These investigators compared systems in which the bridge between the two phenyl groups was either absent or was formed by a sulfur, a $-CH_2-CH_2-$, a $-CH_2CH=$, an oxygen, or a bond between the two carbons in the phenyl group. They discovered that high potency occurred with tricyclic compounds in which the phenyl groups were held at considerable angles to one another (e.g., either imipramine or amitriptyline). Intermediate potency occurred with tricyclic drugs in which the two phenyl groups were held at slight angles or where there was no bridge between the diphenyl systems at all. Those tricyclic drugs in which the phenyl rings were coplanar, such as carbazol, were only weakly active in blocking norepinephrine uptake. They also noted that the demethylated secondary amines were more potent in blocking uptake of norepinephrine than were the drugs having a tertiary amine. The results of these and subsequent investigations were generally consistent, particularly as to the effects of the tertiary vs the secondary tricyclic amines.

It should be noted that much of the above and other earlier work was done with imipramine and desmethylimipramine and, as such, the frequent assumption that these findings can be completely generalized to the amitriptyline-nortriptyline pair needs to be examined carefully. This issue assumes special importance in light of recent evidence suggesting that there may be biochemically identifiable subgroups of depressed patients who respond particularly well to amitriptyline and not imipramine, whereas other groups of patients may have favorable responses to imipramine but not amitriptyline. The next section, then, will deal with the pharmacological data on the theoretical modes of action of the tricyclic antidepressants.

STUDIES OF THE EFFECTS OF DIFFERENT TRICYCLIC DRUGS ON BRAIN AMINE UPTAKE

Biochemistry of Imipramine and Its Demethylated Product

Ross and Renyi[10] published data dealing with the effects of imipramine and demethylation of imipramine upon the uptake of 5-HT, NE, and DA. In this study, they incubated slices of mouse cerebral cortex with different concentrations of the tricyclic antidepressants and estimated the concentrations of drug required to inhibit uptake of 5-HT, NE, and DA by 50 percent, i.e., the EC/50. These data are presented in Table 1: when imipramine is demethylated to desmethylimipramine, there is an approximate tenfold increase in the EC/50 for the blockade of the uptake of 5-HT. Conversely, demethylation of imipramine is accompanied by an approximate tenfold decrement in the EC/50 for the blockade of the uptake of NE. Result: while imipramine is approximately equipotent in blocking the uptake of 5-HT and NE, demethylation produces a drug which is 100-fold more potent in blocking the uptake of NE vis-a-vis 5-HT.

Carlsson[11] has published similar data as to the concentrations of imipramine or desmethylimipramine of 5-HT necessary to give a 50 percent inhibition of uptake by cerebral slices. His results are similar to those of Ross and Renyi for the imipramine-desmethylimipramine pair.

Alpers and Himwich[12] also reported data on uptake of labelled 5-HT by rabbit brain stem slices indicating that amitriptyline and imipramine are approximately equipotent in blocking the uptake of 5-HT, whereas demethylation of imipramine to desmethylimipramine results in tenfold increase in EC/50.

Biochemistry of Amitriptyline and Nortriptyline

While the effects of demethylating imipramine on uptake of 5-HT and NE are thus consistent among investigators, an examination of the data in Table 1 as well as that presented by Carlsson and Alpers and Himwich indicates that the situation is not necessarily the same for amitriptyline and nortriptyline. For example, Table 1 shows that the concentrations of amitriptyline and nortriptyline which are necessary to produce a 50 percent blockade of uptake of 5-HT are not so discrepant. Further, it is apparent that the question of the effects of amitriptyline and nortriptyline on noradrenergic systems was not adequately studied in this earlier work.

Carlsson et al.[13,14] later approached this question via the use of 4-alpha-dimethyl metatyramine (H77/77) and 4-methyl-alpha-ethyl metatyramine (H75/12) as follows: H77/77 is an experimental drug which can enter the brain and displace central catecholamine stores, whereas H75/12 depletes the brain of catecholamine and serotonin (5-HT) stores. Carlsson reasoned that these drugs might utilize the reserpine resistant uptake mechanism at the level of the nerve cell membrane (i.e., the site at which the tricyclic antidepressants are active) and, as such, it might be possible to dissect the differential effects of the tricyclic antidepressants on blocking biogenic amine uptake into DA, NE, and 5-HT neurons.

Table 1.			
	5-HT	NE	DA
Amitriptyline	2×10^{-6}M		
Nortriptyline	5×10^{-6}		
Imipramine	6×10^{-7}	2×10^{-7}M	2×10^{-5}M
Desmethylimipramine	4×10^{-6}	3×10^{-8}	5×10^{-5}

Summary of Biochemical Data

It was found that amitriptyline, nortriptyline, and imipramine were all potent in their ability to block the H75/12-induced depletion of serotonin, whereas the EC/50 for desmethylimipramine was greater than or equal to 50 mg/kg. In contrast, imipramine, amitriptyline, and nortriptyline showed only slight, but significant, effect in blocking the depletion of brain norepinephrine, whereas desmethylimipramine is more effective. It was also noted that desmethylimipramine is ineffective in blocking the depletion of brain DA by H77/77.

Other Methodology:
The Fluorescence Histochemical Technique

In addition to the above biochemical data, the effects of H75/12 on brain 5-HT with and without tricyclic drugs were examined using a histochemical fluorescence method. It was found that amitriptyline, nortriptyline, and imipramine had moderate to marked effects in blocking the depleting effects of this experimental drug; in general, the effects of desmethylimipramine were absent.

Similarly, when a fluorescence histochemical technique was used to examine the actions of these drugs on noradrenergic systems within the brain, it was found that amitriptyline, nortriptyline, and imipramine were relatively ineffective, whereas desmethylimipramine was quite potent.

The results of these studies are consistent with previous data which indicate that imipramine becomes less active on 5-HT neurons and more active with noradrenergic neurons when it is demethylated, but there is serious question as to whether or not such results can be generalized to amitriptyline. It would appear that amitriptyline and its demethylated product (nortriptyline) are approximately equipotent in their effects on 5-HT neurons and ineffective with noradrenergic neurons.

Lidbrink et al.[15] approached the possible differential actions of the tricyclic antidepressants on blocking amine uptake in the central nervous system by pretreating rats with a monoamine oxidase (MAO) inhibitor and reserpine, giving intraventricular injections of either 5-HT or NE and examining the effects of the tricyclic drugs on the reappearance of fluorescence in specific neuronal systems. They found that in doses of 15 mg/kg, amitriptyline significantly reduced the fluorescence in 5-HT nerve terminals and cell bodies. In contrast, when NE was injected into the ventricle, it was discovered that amitriptyline had no effect in preventing the accumulation of fluorescence in noradrenergic nerve terminals.

These same authors also examined the effects of a variety of tricyclic antidepressants on the 5-HT-induced increase in the extensor hind limb reflex of spinal sectioned rats pretreated with reserpine and MAO inhibitor. They noted that in doses of 10 mg/kg—but not 5 mg/kg—amitriptyline increased the reflex activity. Using a similar paradigm with the L-DOPA-induced increase in the flexor reflex activity of reserpine plus MAO inhibitor in pretreated animals, they found that doses of 5 or 15 mg/kg amitriptyline had no effect upon this reflex. These data are generally consistent with the previous findings that amitriptyline exerts its effects principally through actions on serotonergic systems and not through actions on noradrenergic systems.

Effects of Tricyclics on Norepinephrine and Dopamine

Schildkraut et al.[16] approached the problem of the actions of amitriptyline and other tricyclic agents by examining the effects of these drugs on the uptake and metabolism of norepinephrine (isotopically labelled) which had been injected into the ventricles of rat brain. At 25 mg/kg dosages, they discovered that desmethylimipramine, imipramine, and nortriptyline were able to block the uptake of norepinephrine, whereas amitriptyline was without effect. There was some shift, however, toward an increase in labelled normetanephrine and a decrease in deaminated catecholamine metabolites with pretreatment with amitriptyline.

Horn et al.[17] examined the effects of a variety of drugs upon the uptake of DA and NE into the synaptosomes prepared from striatum and hypothalamus, respectively. In agreement with the data of others, they found the expected increase in potency in blockage of uptake of NE when imipramine was demethylated to desmethylimipramine, and that both drugs were relatively ineffective in blocking DA uptake into striatal synaptosomes. Similarly, they found that amitriptyline and nortriptyline had relatively little effect on DA striatal reuptake. In contrast to other investigators, however, they found that amitriptyline and nortriptyline had marked effects upon NE uptake into hypothalamic synaptosomes and that demethylation to nortriptyline produced a decrement in activity.

In addition to the actions of amitriptyline and other tricyclic drugs on blockage of NE uptake, the effects of these agents upon adenosine 3', 5'-monophosphate (cAMP) formation and phosphodiesterase activity in the brain have been examined. This approach is of importance because of the possibility that the neurotransmitter activity of NE is mediated via formation of cAMP in the neuron. Amitriptyline and other tricyclic drugs such as imipramine and desmethylimipramine are able to increase the formation of cAMP in guinea pig cerebral slices[18] and to inhibit phosphodiesterase activity.[19] It would appear, however, that these effects are seen only at very high concentrations of the drugs (1×10^{-4}M); hence, the likelihood that these actions occur *in vivo* is questionable.

EFFECTS OF THE TRICYCLIC ANTIDEPRESSANTS ON THE TURNOVER OF BIOGENIC AMINES IN ANIMALS

Pretreatment with Analogs and Enzyme Inhibitors

Corrodi and Fuxe[20] pretreated experimental animals with imipramine and inhibitors of tyrosine hydroxylase or tryptophan hydroxylase and by biochemical and histochemical fluorescence techniques estimated the rates of disappearance of catecholamines and indoleamines. They found that, even with high doses of imipramine, there were no changes in the rate of depletion of NE or DA, whereas there was a significant slowing of the decrease in the disappearance of 5-HT. In later work, Corrodi[21] examined the effects of amitriptyline, chlorimipramine, and nortriptyline on brain 5-HT turnover by assessing the effects of these agents on the depletion of brain 5-HT and the rates of disappearance of fluorescence in serotonergic areas following the administration of a tryptophan hydroxylase inhibitor. They discovered that it was necessary to use extremely high doses to obtain significant slowing of turnover of 5-HT and, even then, the results were very modest.* Using a somewhat different technique

---

*These findings are in contrast to the rather marked effects of some of these drugs in blocking 5-HT uptake as noted in studies cited elsewhere in this chapter.

and approach, Meek and Werdinius[22] found that following the administration of chlorimipramine and probenecid there was a decrease in the rate of accumulation of 5-hydroxyindole acetic acid (5-HIAA) in the brain, which is consistent with and supportive of the earlier suggestion that the imipramine-like drugs slow the turnover of 5-HT.

Pretreatment with Labelled Amines

Schubert et al.[23] approached the problem of turnover time as influenced by the tricyclic drugs by giving labelled tryptophan or tyrosine either as a single pulse or as an infusion and then measuring the amount of labelled 5-HT, DA, or NE which accumulated during the infusion, or by the amount of labelled amine which was found in the brain at some point after the pulse was given. Drugs evaluated were amitriptyline, imipramine, desmethylimipramine, and nortriptyline. It was clear from their data that none of these drugs affected DA accumulation or disappearance. For 5-HT the disappearance was decreased by amitriptyline and imipramine, but was unaltered by desmethylimipramine or nortriptyline. The accumulation of 5-HT was decreased by imipramine but not by the other drugs. In general, these findings may be considered to be consistent with the notion that imipramine slows the turnover of 5-HT, whereas desmethylimipramine or nortriptyline are without effect.

In an investigation of the effects of psychoactive drugs on 5-HT metabolism, Schildkraut et al.[24] noted that when ^{14}C-5-HT was administered by intracisternal injection and imipramine was subsequently injected intraperitoneally (the animals were sacrificed two hours following the injection of the labelled amine), there was a significant increase in levels of ^{14}C-5-HT in those animals which had been treated with imipramine. This finding is consistent with the work noted above which indicates that imipramine results in a slowing of the turnover of brain 5-HT. Schildkraut[25] has also presented data which indicate that the length of time of drug administration is a significant factor in determining potential effects on turnover time of the amine under study. For example, he noted that when rats were given imipramine (10 mg/kg) twice daily for three weeks there appeared to be an increase in the rate of disappearance of ^{3}H-NE from the brain relative to data obtained from more acute experience.

Pretreatment with Labelled Amine Precursors

Glowinski and co-workers,[26] using a technique which was described earlier in this chapter, examined the effects of some tricyclic antidepressants on the synthesis of NE, DA, and 5-HT from labelled precursors. They discovered that the total labelled 5-HT found (media and tissue) was decreased if imipramine was present in the media or if tissue was obtained from animals which had been pretreated with this drug. Desmethylimipramine produced marked increases in NE synthesis in slices of medulla, but no effects on the synthesis of DA in striatum were noted.

Interpretation of Data

In general, the data regarding effects of tricyclic antidepressants on the turnover of biogenic amines within the brain are less consistent than those which have been obtained from studies of effects of these same drugs on reuptake processes. There is agreement, however, that none of the drugs is effective in altering turnover of brain DA. Although there are some exceptions, it would also appear that amitriptyline and imipramine administration produce a slowing of turnover of 5-HT in the central nervous system.

The effects of other drugs on other amine systems are contradictory. Perhaps this is to be expected because of the fact that experiments which require samples to be obtained over time are difficult to perform in conjunction with dosage-type studies. Furthermore, many of the techniques which are available for assessing turnover time are themselves influenced by administration of the tricyclic drugs. For example, alpha-methyl-paratyrosine, an inhibitor of tyrosine hydroxylase (the rate-limiting enzymatic step in the synthesis of catecholamines), is frequently used to assess the turnover time of NE and DA. But the uptake of this analog of tyrosine is probably altered by desmethylimipramine and, hence, the interpretation of turnover times obtained with the use of this agent becomes difficult.

Further studies which rely on the rate of disappearance of labelled NE or 5-HT following intraventricular injection for estimating turnover time will, of course, be altered by pretreatment with one of the drugs.

EFFECTS OF TRICYCLICS ON NEURONAL SYSTEMS

In the preceding sections, the effects of the tricyclic drugs on the uptake processes and turnover of biogenic amines have been noted and summarized. It is quite apparent from these studies that in many cases inferences as to the actions of these drugs on neuronal function require a number of assumptions. For this reason, studies dealing directly with the effects of these drugs upon the functional activity of specific neurons are of particular interest.

Tricyclics and Midbrain Firing Rate

The first of these studies was done by Sheard et al.[27] These investigators recorded from the dorsal midbrain raphe region which contains the cell bodies of origin of serotonin-containing neurons. Baseline firing rate of these neurons was noted first, and then animals were injected with either amitriptyline, imipramine, or desmethylimipramine. Drugs were given either by the intravenous route in doses varying from 0.5 to 2.5 mg/kg, or via the intraperitoneal route in doses ranging from 1 to 15 mg/kg. They found that amitriptyline and imipramine produced a clear decrement in the rate of firing of the raphe cells, whereas desmethylimipramine was without effect. Further, they noted that if the rats were first pretreated with parachlorophenylalanine (which depletes the brain of 5-HT), imipramine and amitriptyline did not inhibit the raphe unit firing rate.

Samanin et al.[28] noted that the increase in brain 5-HIAA which occurs with stimulation of the raphe nuclei was completely blocked by imipramine but not by desmethylimipramine in a dose of 5 mg/kg. They suggest that this effect may occur because the 5-HT which is released on stimulation is prevented from being taken up and metabolized by monoamine oxidase within the cell.

Tricyclics and Noradrenergic Cells

Nyback et al.[29] examined the effects of tricyclic antidepressants upon the firing rate of brain noradrenergic neurons. These investigators recorded from the locus caeruleus in rats (a small area in the dorsal tectum of the pons containing cell bodies of noradrenergic origin which project forward to several areas of the brain, including the cerebral mantle). The rationale behind this approach is that an increase in the norepinephrine available to noradrenergic receptors would produce, via a neuronal negative feedback system, a decrement in firing of locus caeruleus cells. If, for example, tricyclic drugs do indeed block the uptake of NE at functionally important sites, this should manifest itself in a decrement in the rate of locus caeruleus cell firing rate. Using this technique, the mean dose of drug required to produce a 50 percent inhibition of the baseline firing rate of locus caeruleus cells was determined and these mean values were: desmethylimipramine 0.19 mg/kg, imipramine 0.50 mg/kg, nortriptyline 0.6 mg/kg, and amitriptyline 1.41 mg/kg. It is thus apparent from these data that amitriptyline is the least effective of the four tricyclics in producing a decrement in the firing rate of the locus caeruleus cells. Furthermore, it is clear that while the secondary amine desmethylimipramine is the most potent in producing such an effect, imipramine and nortriptyline are of equal potency to each other.

Table 2.			
	5-HT	NE	DA
Amitriptyline	++++	+	0
Nortriptyline	++	++	0
Imipramine	+++	++	0
Desmethylimipramine	0	++++	0
d-Amphetamine	0	+++	+++

SUMMARY OF THE BASIC NEUROPHARMACOLOGY OF SOME OF THE TRICYCLIC DRUGS

Table 2 summarizes the animal and *in vitro* studies which have been noted thus far dealing with the effects of the tricyclic antidepressants upon the uptake of biogenic amines, turnover times, and functional activity. Several significant points are:

1. In general, it appears that amitriptyline, nortriptyline, imipramine, and desmethylimipramine may not have significant effects upon dopamine systems.

2. In almost all studies, desmethylimipramine has been found to be a potent blocker of the uptake of norepinephrine.

3. It appears that amitriptyline may have the least effect in blocking the uptake of norepinephrine.

4. Nortriptyline (a metabolite of amitriptyline) appears to block norepinephrine uptake. The most persuasive argument for this is the work of Nyback et al.[29] Until this report, the data were contradictory. This report indicates that imipramine and nortriptyline are approximately equipotent on norepinephrine systems *in vivo*.

5. The data regarding the effects of imipramine upon the blockade of the uptake of NE are somewhat contradictory: most studies indicate that imipramine does block the uptake of NE, but there are some exceptions, such as the reports of Carlsson et al. [13,14]

6. It seems that both amitriptyline and imipramine may have significant effects on 5-HT systems, whereas desmethylimipramine may not.

7. Reasonably close scrutiny of the available data suggests that nortriptyline produces a blockade in the uptake of 5-HT. (This finding is often obscured by generalizations regarding the actions of tertiary and secondary tricyclic amines.)

STUDIES OF THE EFFECTS OF AMITRIPTYLINE AND OTHER TRICYCLIC ANTIDEPRESSANTS ON THE METABOLISM AND DISPOSITION OF BIOGENIC AMINES IN MAN

Pharmacological Actions of the Drugs on Amine Metabolism

In an initial report, Bowers et al.[30] noted that patients who were being treated with amitriptyline had significant reductions in cerebrospinal fluid (CSF) 5-HIAA during the period of treatment relative to a baseline period. In contrast, no significant differences in homovanillic acid concentration during the two periods were seen.

Papeschi and McClure[31] also noted similar significant decreases in CSF 5-HIAA but not homovanillic acid following two weeks of imipramine treatment. Åsberg et al.[32] found that 5-HIAA as well as IAA levels in the CSF of depressed patients were decreased as a consequence of treatment with nortriptyline.

Bowers[33] further found that while the levels of L-tryptophan in the CSF before and during treatment were the same, there was a decreased accumulation of 5-HIAA during treatment with amitriptyline.

These data were interpreted as being compatible with the possibility that during treatment with amitriptyline, central 5-HT turnover was decreased.

In a similar study, Post and Goodwin[34] noted that the treatment of patients with amitriptyline or imipramine was associated with a decreased accumulation of 5-HIAA in CSF. They found no differences for homovanillic acid. These findings, as those of Bowers,[33] suggest that amitriptyline and imipramine produce a decrement in turnover of serotonin within the central nervous system.

Effects of tricyclics on catecholamine turnover: Three separate groups of investigators[35,36,37] have also demonstrated that treatment of patients with imipramine results in marked decrements in the excretion of vanillylmandelic acid and in two reports it was noted that this decrement was accompanied by a large increase in the excretion of normetanephrine. The experimental approaches in these later investigations did not allow definitive interpretations as to the mechanisms which might be involved although it appeared that a decrement in overall synthesis of catecholamines might be being produced by imipramine. In this regard, however, the recent work of Roth and Gillis[38] should be noted. These workers have found that imipramine is able to inhibit *in vitro* monoamine oxidase of the B type. It is thus possible that the changes in catecholamine and 5-HT metabolite levels which occur with treatment with these drugs may be being produced in part via monoamine oxidase inhibition.

Depression as a Biochemical Disorder: Therapeutic Response and Effects of Tricyclic Drugs

Relation of MHPG excretion:* In addition to the above general pharmacological effects of the drug, there are some preliminary data available on a small number of patients which suggest that the changes in amine metabolism and/or disposition

*D,L-4-hydroxy-3-methoxyphenylglycol

which occur with treatment with the tricyclic drugs may vary with the response of the patient to the particular drug. As an example, Maas et al.[37] reported that patients who responded well to imipramine or desmethylimipramine had low pretreatment 24-hour urinary MHPG and that when MHPG was assayed during the fourth week of treatment with these drugs, the level of MHPG in the urine showed modest increments or no change. In marked contrast were those patients who had normal or high urinary MHPG, i.e., these patients tended not to respond to imipramine or desmethylimipramine, and during the fourth week of treatment there was a marked decrement in urinary MHPG. While pretreatment normetanephrine was not associated with response to imipramine or desmethylimipramine, those patients who responded particularly well to imipramine or desmethylimipramine had marked increases in normetanephrine during the fourth week of treatment relative to baseline periods, whereas this was less noticeable with those patients who responded less well. Schildkraut's[39] findings in a preliminary study suggest that high or normal baseline urinary MHPG is associated with a favorable response to amitriptyline. A study by Beckman et al.[40] lends support to the findings of Maas and Schildkraut. However, these findings are, of course, preliminary in nature and require further investigation.

Cerebrospinal fluid and indoles: Åsberg et al.[32] also made the observation that while as a group nortriptyline produced a decrement in 5-HIAA and IAA in CSF, if one looked at the patients in terms of those having low vs high CSF 5-HIAA levels, a different pattern emerged. In seven of the patients who had pretreatment 5-HIAA levels below 15 ng/ml of CSF, the 5-HIAA concentration increased in five patients and decreased in two. In contrast, in the 13 patients with an initial 5-HIAA concentration higher than 15 ng/ml the 5-HIAA levels decreased in all.

The last studies cited are of interest not only because they suggest that depression is a biochemically heterogeneous illness, but also because they indicate that the type of biological response that one obtains with treatment with a particular drug may change as a function of the type of biochemistry which may underlie the illness.

Summary: The available data from man are generally consistent with that obtained from animals and *in vitro*, i.e., there is an apparent lack of effect on DA systems by amitriptyline, nortriptyline, and imipramine, and a clear effect by these agents on 5-HT systems. Less information regarding central nervous system NE metabolism as it is influenced by these drugs is available, but it is anticipated that much information in this area will be available in the near future.

CONCLUDING COMMENTS

In all of the cited animal and clinical studies, emphasis has been upon the changes in metabolism or disposition of particular biogenic amines following administration of a particular drug. Unfortunately, the *in vivo* situation with amitriptyline and imipramine is such that the direct extrapolation from *in vitro* or acute experiments in animals to the situation in man cannot be made. This is so not only because of the difference which may be obtained in the chronic vs the acute situation but, more importantly, because both amitriptyline and imipramine are demethylated to the secondary amines.

Further, the rate of this demethylation and/or metabolism via ring hydroxylation to inactive compounds not only varies from subject to subject but apparently differs for amitriptyline and imipramine. For example, the available data would indicate that imipramine is relatively rapidly converted to desmethylimipramine and the ratios of desmethylimipramine to imipramine are far greater than unity. In contrast, the studies which have been done with amitriptyline indicate that the ratios of amitriptyline to nortriptyline might be approximately unity.[41,42]

Finally, most of the drugs are bound to protein in plasma and it is only the free unbound drug which can penetrate the brain and is available to act as a therapeutic agent. The relationship of the free vs the bound amine and the ratios of the tertiary to the secondary amines of the amitriptyline-nortriptyline type or the imipramine - desmethylimipramine type are obviously areas which are going to require further investigation.

REFERENCES

1. Schildkraut, J.J.: The catecholamine hypothesis of affective disorders: A review of supporting evidence, Amer. J. Psychiat. 122:509, 1965.

2. Bunney, W.E., Jr. and Davis, J.M.: Norepinephrine in depressive reactions, Arch. Gen. Psychiat. 13:483, 1965.

3. Schildkraut, J.J. and Kety, S.S.: Biogenic amines and emotion, Science 156:21, 1967.

4. Glowinski, J. and Axelrod, J.: Inhibition of uptake of tritiated-noradrenaline in the intact rat brain by imipramine and structurally related compounds, Nature 204:1318, 1964.

5. Bickel, M.H. and Brodie, B.B.: Structure and antidepressant activity of imipramine analogues, Int. J. Neuropharmacol. 3:611, 1964.

6. Maxwell, R.A., Chaplin, E., Eckhardt, S.B., Soares, J.R. and Hite, G.: Conformational similarities between molecular models of phenethylamine and of potent inhibitors of the uptake of tritiated norepinephrine by adrenergic nerves in rabbit aorta, J. Pharmacol. Exp. Ther. 173:158, 1970.

7. Maxwell, R.A., Eckhardt, S.B. and Hite, G.: Kinetic and thermodynamic considerations regarding the inhibition by tricyclic antidepressants of the uptake of tritiated norepinephrine by the adrenergic nerves in rabbit aortic strips, J. Pharmacol. Exp. Ther. 171:62, 1970.

8. Maxwell, R.A., Keenan, P.D., Chaplin, E., Roth, B. and Eckhardt, S.B.: Molecular features affecting the potency of tricyclic antidepressants and structurally related compounds as inhibitors of the uptake of tritiated norepinephrine by rabbit aortic strips, J. Pharmacol. Exp. Ther. 166:320, 1969.

9. Salama, A.I., Insalaco, J.R. and Maxwell, R.A.: Concerning the molecular requirements for the inhibition of the uptake of racemic ^{3}H-norepinephrine into rat cerebral cortex slices by tricyclic antidepressants and related compounds, J. Pharmacol. Exp. Ther. 178:474, 1971.

10. Ross, S.B. and Renyi, A.L.: Inhibition of the uptake of tritiated catecholamines by antidepressant and related agents, European J. Pharmacol. 2:181, 1967.

11. Carlsson, A.: Structural specificity for inhibition of [^{14}C]-5-hydroxytryptamine uptake by cerebral slices, J. Pharm. Pharmac. 22:729, 1970.

12. Alpers, H.S. and Himwich, H.E.: An *in vitro* study of the effects of tricyclic antidepressant drugs on the accumulation of C^{14}-serotonin by rabbit brain, Biol. Psychiat. 1:81, 1969.

13. Carlsson, A., Corrodi, H., Fuxe, K. and Hökfelt, T.: Effect of antidepressant drugs on the depletion of intraneuronal brain 5-hydroxytryptamine stores caused by 4-methyl-α-ethyl-meta-tyramine, European J. Pharmacol. 5:357, 1969.

14. Carlsson, A., Corrodi, H., Fuxe, K. and Hökfelt, T.: Effects of some antidepressant drugs on the depletion of intraneuronal brain catecholamine stores caused by 4,α-dimethyl-meta-tyramine, European J. Pharmacol. 5:367, 1969.

15. Lidbrink, P., Jonsson, G. and Fuxe, K.: The effect of imipramine-like drugs and antihistamine drugs on uptake mechanisms in the central noradrenaline and 5-hydroxytryptamine neurons, Neuropharmacol. 10:521, 1971.

16. Schildkraut, J.J., Dodge, G.A. and Logue, M.A.: Effects of tricyclic antidepressants on the uptake and metabolism of intracisternally administered norepineprhine-H^3 in rat brain, J. Psychiat. Res. 7:29, 1969.

17. Horn, A.S., Coyle, J.T. and Snyder, S.H.: Catecholamine uptake by synaptosomes from rat brain, Molecular Pharmacology 7:66, 1970.

18. Kodama, T., Matsukado, Y., Suzuki, T., Tanaka, S. and Shimizu, H.: Stimulated formation of adenosine 3′,5′-monophosphate by desipramine in brain slices, Biochimica et Biophysica Acta 252:165, 1971.

19. Ramsden, E.N.: Cyclic A.M.P. in depression and mania, Lancet 2:108, 1970.

20. Corrodi, H. and Fuxe, K.: The effect of imipramine on central monoamine neurons, J. Pharm. Pharmacol. 20:230, 1968.

21. Corrodi, H. and Fuxe, K.: Decreased turnover in central 5-HT nerve terminals induced by antidepressant drugs of the imipramine type, European J. Pharmacol. 7:56, 1969.

22. Meek, J. and Werdinius, B.: Hydroxytryptamine turnover decreased by the antidepressant drug chlorimipramine, J. Pharm. Pharmacol. 22:141, 1970.

23. Schubert, J., Nybäck, H. and Sedvall, G.: Effect of antidepressant drugs on accumulation and disappearance of monoamines formed in vivo from labelled precursors in mouse brain, J. Pharm. Pharmacol. 22:136, 1970.

24. Schildkraut, J.J., Schanberg, S.M., Breese, G.R. and Kopin, I.J.: Effects of psychoactive drugs on the metabolism of intracisternally administered serotonin in rat brain, Biochem. Pharmacol. 18:1971, 1969.

25. Schildkraut, J.J., Winokur, A. and Applegate, C.W.: Norepinephrine turnover and metabolism in rat brain after long-term administration of imipramine, Science 168:867, 1970.

26. Glowinski, J.: Release of monoamines in the central nervous system. In New Aspects of Storage and Release Mechanisms of CA, ed. H.J. Schumann and G. Kroneberg, Berlin, Heidelberg, Springer-Verlag, 1970, pp. 237-251.

27. Sheard, M.H., Zolovick, A. and Aghajanian, G.K.: Raphe neurons: effect of tricyclic antidepressant drugs, Brain Research 43:690, 1972.

28. Samanin, R., Ghezzi, D. and Garattini, S: Effect of imipramine and desipramine on the metabolism of serotonin in midbrain raphe stimulated rats, European J. Pharmacol. 20:281, 1972.

29. Nyback, H.V., Walters, J.R., Aghajanian, G.K. and Roth, R.H.: Tricyclic antidepressants: Effects on the firing rate of brain noradrenergic neurons, European J. Pharmacol. In press.

30. Bowers, M.B., Jr., Heninger, G.R. and Gerbode, F.: Cerebrospinal fluid 5-hydroxyindoleacetic acid and homovanillic acid in psychiatric patients, Int. J. Neuropharmacol. 8:255, 1969.

31. Papeschi, R. and McClure, D.J.: Homovanillic and 5-hydroxyindoleacetic acid in cerebrospinal fluid of depressed patients, Arch. Gen. Psychiat. 25:354, 1971.

32. Åsberg, M., Bertilsson, L., Tuck, D., Cronholm, B. and Sjöqvist, F.: Indole-amine metabolites in the cerebrospinal fluid of depressed patients before and during treatment with nortriptyline, Clin. Pharmacol. Ther. 14:277, 1973.

33. Bowers, M.B., Jr.: Amitriptyline in man: Decreased formation of central 5-hydroxyindoleacetic acid, Clin. Pharmacol. Ther. 15:167, 1974.

34. Post, R.M. and Goodwin, F.K.: Effects of amitriptyline and imipramine on amine metabolites in the cerebrospinal fluid of depressed patients, Arch. Gen. Psychiat. 30:234, 1974.

35. Schildkraut, J.J., Gordon, E.K. and Durell, J.: Catecholamine metabolism in affective disorders: I. normetanephrine and VMA excretion in depressed patients treated with imipramine, J. Psychiat. Res. 3:213, 1965.

36. Prange, A.J., Jr., Wilson, I.C., Knox, A.E., McClane, T.K., Breese, G.R., Martin, B.R., Alltop, L.B. and Lipton, M.A.: Thyroid-imipramine interaction: Clinical results and basic mechanism. In *Brain Chemistry and Mental Disease,* ed. B.T. Ho and W. M. McIsaac, New York, Plenum Press, Inc., 1971, p. 208.

37. Maas, J.W., Fawcett, J.A. and Dekirmenjian, H.: Catecholamine metabolism, depressive illness, and drug response, Arch. Gen. Psychiat. 26:252, 1972.

38. Roth, J.A. and Gillis, C.N.: Inhibition of lung, liver and brain monoamine oxidase by imipramine and desipramine, Biochem. Pharmacol. 23:1138, 1974.

39. Schildkraut, J.J.: Norepinephrine metabolites as biochemical criteria for classifying depressive disorders and predicting responses to treatment: preliminary findings, Amer. J. Psychiat. 130:695, 1973.

40. Beckman, H., Jones, C.C. and Goodwin, F.R.: Central norepinephrine metabolism and the prediction of antidepressant response to imipramine or amitriptyline. Presented at the Annual Meeting of the American Psychiatric Association, May 1974. In press.

41. Moody, J.P., Tait, A.C. and Todrich, A.: Plasma levels of imipramine and desmethylimipramine during therapy, Brit. J. Psychiat. 113:183, 1967.

42. Braithwaite, R.A. and Widdop, B.: A specific gas-chromatographic method for the measurement of "steady-state" plasma levels of amitriptyline and nortriptyline in patients, Clin. Chim. Acta 35:461, 1971.

EFFECTS OF AMITRIPTYLINE ON SLEEP PATTERNS

ERNEST HARTMANN, M.D.
Director, Sleep and Dream Laboratory
Boston State Hospital
Boston, Massachusetts

Ernest Hartmann, M.D. is Director of the Sleep and Dream Laboratory at Boston State Hospital and Chairman of the Research Ethics Committee at the same institution. He is a member of the FDA Panel on Sedatives, Tranquilizers, and Sleeping-Aids.

In addition, he is Associate Professor of Psychiatry at Tufts University School of Medicine, Lecturer in Psychiatry at Boston University School of Medicine, and a faculty member at Boston Psychoanalytic Institute. Dr. Hartmann has membership in scientific and medical societies and has received much recognition from his peers for his contributions to the practice of psychiatry. He is Associate Editor of *Seminars In Psychiatry,* Consulting Editor of both *Psychophysiology* and *Psychopharmacologia*, and is the author of 130 technical articles and four books.

EFFECTS OF AMITRIPTYLINE ON SLEEP PATTERNS

NORMAL HUMAN SLEEP

Sleep: A Behavioral State

Sleep is basically a behavioral state—a regularly recurrent, easily reversible state characterized by relative quiescence and by great decrease in response to external stimulation. Over the past years, it has been shown that a series of EEG and other polygraphic changes are very closely linked to this behavioral state. The pattern depicted in Figure 1 represents the normal pattern of a night's sleep in a young adult human. The exact definitions of the EEG stages and other details have been reviewed many times.[1,2,3] Some aspects of the pattern are worth mentioning here, however, since they are very constant in normal sleep, but are altered in such conditions as depression and after administration of various drugs.

Sleep Cycles

First of all, the cyclical nature of sleep is prominent and such cycles have been found in almost all mammalian species studied.

In man, there are four or five cycles during the night, lasting 90 to 110 minutes each; the cycles comprise the regular alternation between synchronized (S) sleep, also called non-REM sleep or orthodox sleep, and desynchronized (D) sleep, also called dreaming-sleep, REM sleep, or paradoxical sleep. Another important regular feature is that S-sleep always precedes D-sleep, and the first D-period does not generally occur for 80 to 100 minutes after sleep onset. D-time comprises about 100 minutes per night in the young adult. Stages 3 and 4 sleep, also called slow-wave sleep, are the deeper portions of S-sleep and occur almost entirely at the beginning of the night. Slow-wave sleep occupies 60 to 120 minutes per night in a young adult; it is longer in the child, and diminishes rapidly with increasing age. Although not indicated in Figure 1, the young adult frequently has two or three brief arousals or awakenings during the night.

SLEEP PATTERNS
IN DEPRESSED PATIENTS

It has long been known clinically that alterations in sleep patterns occur in depression, as well as in mania and certain other mental illnesses. Sleep laboratory studies of recent years have begun to elucidate the exact nature of the sleep alterations.[4-13] The first impression one gets in reading studies of sleep in depressed patients is that there is great variation with no clear-cut single pattern emerging. Many patients, for instance, have greatly shortened sleep while some have increased sleep; some have obviously disturbed-looking sleep, full of awakenings, but some do not. A whole range of results has been reported on amounts of D-time and most other variables during sleep. A decrease in slow-wave sleep, especially Stage 4, is very frequently, but not always, reported. However, if one looks more carefully, I believe that two identifiable patterns of altered sleep begin to emerge, and that one can organize most findings around these two types of disturbed sleep patterns.

Pattern I: Disturbed Sleep

One pattern of sleep disturbance in depression can be summarized as "poor sleep": reduced total sleep time, frequent awakenings during the night, early morning awakenings, and definite subjective dissatisfaction with sleep. In the sleep laboratory, total sleep time is definitely reduced. A total sleep time of 4 to 6 hours is usually recorded in these patients. It is impossible to give precise figures for this hypothetical group because the studies usually present overall means, and do not differentiate between the different sleep patterns in depression. Stages 3 and 4 sleep are clearly reduced in this group and take up from 0 to 50 percent of their normal values. Waking time after sleep onset is clearly increased; waking during the night and "early morning awakenings" cannot be clearly differentiated but both are almost always elevated. D-time is usually but not invariably decreased. There is usually an increase not only in waking time and number of awakenings but also in body movements during the night and in stage shifts, especially shifts to lighter Stage 1 or 2 sleep. Finally, one study by Zung[14] has shown that arousal threshold from a given stage is significantly lower in depressed patients so that even when these patients do manifest a given stage on the EEG, they are more easily aroused from that stage than is a normal subject.* All these EEG findings certainly seem to indicate that the patient is fully justified in his impression that he is sleeping poorly.

Summarizing the above, one could say that the decrease in deep slow-wave sleep, the increase in waking and in the number of awakenings and stage shifts, and the decrease in arousal threshold of pattern I could all be considered measures of increased arousal continuing during sleep (and perhaps could be related neurophysiologically to overactivity of the reticular activating system).

This first pattern of sleep disturbance corresponds somewhat to the most frequently described pattern in textbooks and appears to be frequent among severely depressed or psychotically depressed hospitalized patients.

---

*Zung did not classify depressed patients the way we are doing here, but it is clear from his data that he is referring chiefly to the first type of sleep alteration.

Pattern II: Hypersomnia

There is also a very different pattern of sleep alteration which has been occasionally mentioned in the literature for many years, but which in my opinion emerges quite clearly from recent sleep studies. This pattern is characterized by normal or somewhat increased sleep, i.e., hypersomnia, and sleep which is clinically not particularly disturbed. Laboratory studies show normal or increased total sleep time, and little or no sleep disturbance in terms of increased latency, increased awakenings during the night, or increased stage shifts. There is sometimes but not always a decrease in slow-wave sleep. D-time is usually increased, and D-periods occur early in the night and the early D-periods are generally long and "intense," i.e., with many rapid eye movements per time unit.

Sleep pattern II is found more frequently than had been suspected. First of all, my impressions from a large number of interviews and studies of "long sleepers" have suggested that persons with mild or neurotic depressions, especially young subjects, frequently respond to the depression by increased sleep time.[15,16,17] A large-scale attempt to establish, within subjects, at what periods of their lives they seem to require more sleep or less sleep came to similar conclusions: periods of depressions were among the periods when more sleep was definitely required.[17] Thus a mild depressed state is frequently associated with hypersomnia, and laboratory investigations suggest that this hypersomnia is associated with especially high D-time whereas slow-wave sleep is not increased.[15] However, sleep pattern II is not restricted to mild depression; it has been found in certain very severely depressed patients, and especially among manic-depressive patients.[5,18]

In my opinion, pattern II is not merely associated with less severe depression but may represent a different biological form of the depressive syndrome. Thus, in a group of manic-depressive patients studied over long periods, we found that sleep time and D-time were higher during very depressed periods than during mildly depressed periods.

Coexistence of Patterns I and II

The two patterns may also exist at different times within the same individual. Snyder, although he has not specifically discussed the second pattern, has suggested that when hypersomnia and high D-time are found in the depressed patient, it is during a stage of partial recovery, i.e., when there has been previous sleep deprivation or D-deprivation. I have suggested rather that pattern II is perhaps more typical of depression in general, ranging from very mild almost normal depressions to the more severe ones, i.e., that there is an increased requirement for sleep and for D-time in depression, but that certain severely depressed patients have an additional deficit in their sleep-waking mechanisms or arousal mechanisms making it impossible to get to sleep. It should be noted that the two patterns are *not* opposites, i.e., hyposomnia versus hypersomnia. The second pattern can be seen as an increased requirement for sleep and for D-sleep especially, whereas the first pattern is by no means a decreased requirement but rather an inability to sleep (despite quite possibly a high bodily requirement), thus helping produce the acute distress and dissatisfaction with sleep characteristic of the first group.

AMITRIPTYLINE EFFECTS ON SLEEP: CLINICAL IMPRESSIONS

Amitriptyline has been used widely in the treatment of depression in recent years and, in addition to a few studies of sleep to be reviewed below, some general clinical impressions have emerged as to its effects on sleep. First of all, it appears that amitriptyline has a definite hypnotic or drowsiness-inducing effect most prominent when first given [see, for instance, Dobkin,[19] Allen et al.[20]], and this effect appears to be greater after amitriptyline than after imipramine, certainly greater than with monoamine oxidase inhibitors. This hypnotic effect has been noted anecdotally in normal subjects as well as in depressed patients and usually is most prominent during the first few days of administration. Secondly, it is clear that in depressed patients who are improving on amitriptyline, usually patients with pattern I (severely disturbed) sleep, sleep patterns clearly improve along with the improvement in depression. Sleep lengthens, awakenings are reduced, and subjective feelings about sleep improve. These effects usually occur after approximately two weeks of drug administration and one cannot, of course, be certain whether the sleep changes are a direct amitriptyline effect or secondary to the improvement in the depression. Similar gradual sleep changes are found when depression improves spontaneously or after other treatment modalities.

AMITRIPTYLINE EFFECTS ON SLEEP: CLINICAL NONLABORATORY STUDIES

There is one study by Urbach[21] comparing the hypnotic effects of placebo, amitriptyline, and secobarbital on sleep in non-insomniac hospitalized patients awaiting surgery. Sleep was rated on many different measures by the patient himself, and an interviewer also rated the patient's appearance, alertness, etc. in the morning. The patients reported their sleep as better and reported a shorter sleep latency on any of the three doses of amitriptyline studied (25, 50, or 75 mg) than on placebo. However, the higher doses of amitriptyline produced a less refreshed feeling in the morning. The interviewer's ratings showed that the placebo patients appeared more "worried" or "tense" in the morning whereas the patients on high doses of amitriptyline appeared more "sleepy." The author concludes that in this group of patients "amitriptyline definitely improved the quality of sleep as compared to placebo." While sleep was better following any of the active medications than after placebo, secobarbital 200 mg was followed by the best results and differed significantly compared to the three amitriptyline dosages and 100 mg of secobarbital.

AMITRIPTYLINE EFFECTS ON SLEEP:
LABORATORY STUDIES

Introduction

We have recently completed a series of studies on the effects of long-term administration of various psychotropic drugs including amitriptyline on normal sleep.[22,23,24] Fourteen normal subjects were involved. These subjects were studied for a total of 1125 nights of recorded laboratory sleep. Subjects were normal males, ages 21 to 35. Each was involved in six 60-day study periods, one for each of the following drug conditions in a balanced design: placebo; reserpine 0.50 mg daily; amitriptyline 50 mg daily; chlorpromazine 50 mg daily; chloral hydrate 500 mg daily; and chlordiazepoxide 50 mg daily. Subjects, experimenters who ran the studies at night, and assistants who scored the records were all blind to drug condition.

During each 60-day period, the subject took a single pink capsule (drug or placebo) 20 minutes before bedtime every night for 28 nights, and then no medication for approximately 32 nights. Subjects slept in the laboratory the first 5 nights on medication, then once a week for the remainder of the medication period, then the first 6 nights after discontinuation of medication, then once a week for the remainder of the discontinuation period.

Subjects filled out a sleep log every morning throughout the study whether they slept at home or in the laboratory. They filled in time to bed, time up, estimate of time slept, any dreams, any unusual events or side effects, and then were asked to rate on a simple 5-point scale both the quality of their sleep for the night and how they felt that morning. Subjects filled out an adjective checklist—The Psychiatric Outpatient Mood Scale (POMS)— once per week throughout the study, and were instructed to answer the questions for the entire past week, i.e., how they had tended to feel for that week, not how they were feeling at the time they filled out this form.

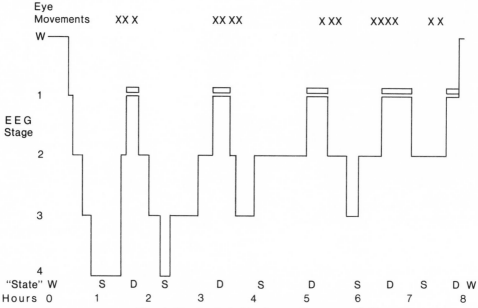

Fig. 1. Typical night sleep of young adult

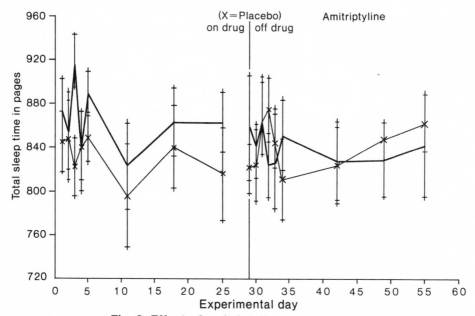

Fig. 2. Effect of amitriptyline on total sleep time

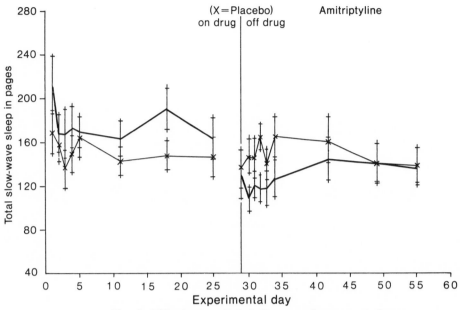

Fig. 3. Effect of amitriptyline on slow-wave sleep

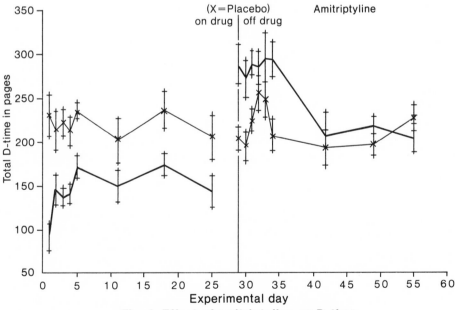

Fig. 4. Effect of amitriptyline on D-time

Table 1. Amitriptyline: Effects on laboratory sleep

	On medication				
	First night	First 3 nights	First 5 nights	Remaining nights	All nights
Time awake (30-sec pages)	29.2 (−16.6)	30.4 (−18.6)	34.7 (−15.0)	40.7 (+2.2)	36.9 (−7.9)
Number of awakenings	3.3 (+0.3)	3.6 (+0.4)	4.0 (+1.0)	3.5 (+1.1)	3.8 (+1.0)
Sleep latency (30-sec pages)	20.4 (−3.5)	18.7 (−4.8)	19.1 (−2.8)	26.3 (+4.1)	21.8 (+0.2)
Total sleep time (30-sec pages)	874 (+28.5)	883 (+43.7)*	875 (+32.9)*	846 (+29.1)	864 (+27.0)
Stage 1 (30-sec pages)	20.3 (−17.0)*	29.8 (−5.9)	33.8 (−3.4)	41.1 (+7.0)	36.6 (+0.4)
Stage 2 (30-sec pages)	550 (+138.2)***	545 (+118.4)***	525 (+97.5)***	486 (+61.0)**	511 (+83.2)***
Stage 3 (30-sec pages)	121.0 (+30.1)	101.5 (+26.7)*	96.9 (+23.5)**	88.1 (+17.2)*	93.6 (+20.4)***
Stage 4 (30-sec pages)	91.9 (+16.6)	81.6 (−0.5)	81.7 (−2.4)	78.5 (+1.8)	80.5 (−1.0)
Slow-wave sleep (30-sec pages)	213 (+46.7)	183 (+26.2)	179 (+21.1)	167 (+18.9)	174 (+19.4)
D-Time (30-sec pages)	91 (−139.4)***	124 (−95.1)***	137 (−82.4)***	153 (−57.7)*	143 (−76.0)***
D-Latency (30-sec pages)	294 (+125.0)	241 (+65.3)*	250 (+77.4)*	255 (+75.1)*	252 (+78.1)**
Number of D-periods	2.5 (−1.5)***	2.8 (−1.2)***	2.9 (−1.1)***	3.0 (−1.0)**	3.0 (−1.1)***
Number of stage shifts	61.2 (+6.8)	58.9 (+3.8)	60.4 (+5.0)	56.5 (+2.0)	59.0 (+3.6)
Cycle length (30-sec pages)	260 (+46.3)	310 (+102.6)***	297 (+89.6)***	232 (+33.4)	272 (+68.8)***
Number of body movements	48.5 (+1.4)	46.6 (−2.2)	45.9 (−2.6)	52.1 (+6.3)	48.2 (+0.7)
Disturbance index	77.7 (−15.2)	77.1 (−20.7)	80.6 (−17.6)	92.8 (+8.3)	85.2 (−7.2)

*$P < 0.05$.   **$P < 0.01$.   ***$P < 0.001$.
Figures in parentheses represent drug value minus placebo value.

Off medication

First night	First 3 nights	Second 3 nights	Remaining nights	Last night
50.8 (+0.4)	58.3 (+19.7)*	58.4 (+19.8)*	45.9 (−4.2)	38.3 (−8.3)
4.5 (+1.6)	4.7 (+1.3)	3.7 (+0.6)	2.4 (−0.6)	1.3 (−1.3)
24.9 (+7.2)	27.1 (+7.3)*	23.3 (+2.0)	21.4 (−10.8)	16.7 (−14.1)
858 (+34.8)	855 (+17.3)	832 (−11.2)	836 (−3.9)	850 (−9.9)
46.7 (+19.6)*	37.5 (+5.6)	38.6 (+8.6)*	30.8 (+0.6)	33.9 (+6.4)
391 (−62.2)*	413 (−42.8)*	380 (−28.9)*	456 (+10.4)	475 (+39.2)
73.9 (+12.7)	64.7 (−1.4)	67.2 (+3.6)	63.8 (−1.0)	65.1 (−2.1)
57.1 (−24.9)*	55.5 (−20.7)*	54.2 (−41.9)***	76.2 (−21.3)*	71.4 (−25.5)
131 (−12.2)	120 (−22.1)*	121 (−38.3)***	140 (−22.3)*	136 (−27.6)
289 (+89.6)***	284 (+76.6)***	291 (+47.4)*	209 (+15.2)	204 (−8.1)
146 (−23.2)*	142 (−25.2)*	114 (−25.9)*	160 (−39.2)	186 (−33.8)
4.0 (+0.1)	4.2 (+0.3)	4.6 (+0.4)***	3.9 (+0.1)	3.9 (+0.3)
58.5 (+7.2)	57.3 (+3.7)	55.6 (+0.8)	52.6 (−1.4)	49.2 (−3.6)
228 (+13.2)	218 (+0.2)	197 (−12.5)	218 (+5.2)	212 (−15.3)
46.4 (−1.0)	48.9 (+1.3)	52.2 (+6.8)**	46.8 (−5.3)	53.8 (−3.8)
97.2 (−0.6)	107.2 (+21.0)**	110.6 (+26.6)**	92.7 (−9.4)	92.1 (−4.5)

Time awake: All waking from start to end of EEG recording.

Number of awakenings: Number of periods of waking separated from other periods of waking by at least 5 min of sleep.

Sleep latency: Time spent from start of recording until first Stage 1 which reaches Stage 2.

Total sleep time: Sum of Stages 1−4 and REM; Stages 1−3, and 4.

D-time: Time spent in Stage REM.

D-latency: Total time asleep before the first occurrence of Stage REM.

Number of D-periods: Number of occurrences of Stage REM separated by more than 15 min.

Number of stage shifts: Total number of stage changes.

Cycle length: Average time between ends of D-periods.

Number of body movements: Number of body movements more than 5 sec in length.

Disturbance index: Sum of number of body movements and time awake.

Table 2. Amitriptyline: Effects on home log variables

	On medication				
	First week	Second week	Third week	Fourth week	All weeks
Estimated total sleep time (in hours and tenths)	8.2 (+0.7)**	7.8 (+0.1)	7.9 (+0.5)*	6.6 (+0.5)	7.9 (+0.4)
Quality of sleep (1 = worst to 5 = best)	3.0 (+0.1)	3.0 (+0.0)	2.9 (−0.1)	2.8 (+0.4)	3.0 (+0.0)
How feel in the morning (1 = worst to 5 = best)	2.7 (−0.2)*	2.6 (−0.3)***	2.7 (−0.3)*	2.4 (−0.0)	2.7 (−0.3)***
Feel sick in any way (mean number of positive responses)	0.4 (+0.2)	0.2 (−0.0)	0.3 (+0.2)*	0.4 (+0.4)*	0.3 (+0.2)*
Unusual psychological feelings (mean number of positive responses)	0.1 (+0.0)	0.2 (+0.1)	0.2 (+0.2)	0.3 (+0.3)*	0.2 (+0.1)
Fault of medication (mean number of positive responses—this refers to the two immediately preceding items and was only answered if there was a positive response to either)	0.3 (+0.1)	0.3 (+0.3)*	0.3 (+0.3)*	0.4 (+0.4)*	0.5 (+0.3)*
Psychiatric Outpatient Mood Scale:					
Tension-anxiety	−3.2 (−1.2)	−2.5 (+0.6)	−1.2 (+0.5)	−0.8 (+0.7)	−2.2 (+0.1)
Anger-hostility	−10.5 (−0.5)	−9.2 (+1.4)	−7.5 (+1.5)	−5.1 (+2.6)	−8.8 (+1.2)
Fatigue	0.5 (−6.0)*	1.0 (+6.3)*	1.0 (+6.8)**	1.7 (+5.6)*	1.0 (+6.5)**
Depression	−12.2 (−2.0)	−11.8 (−1.5)	−10.4 (−0.5)	−8.7 (−1.8)	−11.3 (−1.2)
Vigor	6.5 (−1.9)	5.4 (−2.9)	4.5 (−2.9)	3.7 (+1.2)	5.3 (−2.2)
Confusion	−0.3 (+0.0)	−0.4 (−0.2)	0.6 (−0.4)	1.0 (+0.1)	−0.0 (−0.3)

*$P<0.05$.   **$P<0.01$.   ***$P<0.001$.
Figures in parentheses represent drug value minus placebo value.

Off medication				
First week	Second week	Third week	Fourth week	All weeks
7.0 (−0.6)	7.5 (−0.3)	6.6 (−0.2)	6.6 (+0.7)	7.3 (−0.3)
2.9 (−0.0)	2.9 (−0.1)	2.7 (+0.2)*	2.7 (+0.3)	3.0 (+0.0)
2.9 (−0.0)	2.8 (−0.0)	2.5 (+0.0)	2.6 (+0.4)	2.9 (+0.0)
0.1 (+0.1)*	0.1 (+0.1)*	0.1 (+0.0)	0.1 (+0.0)	0.1 (+0.1)
0.2 (+0.2)	0.1 (−0.0)	0.0 (−0.1)	0.0 (−0.1)	0.1 (−0.0)
0.2 (+0.2)	0.0 (−0.0)	0.0 (+0.0)	0.0 (+0.0)	0.2 (+0.2)
−1.9 (−0.4)	−2.4 (−0.9)	−1.4 (+0.9)	−2.2 (+0.5)	−1.9 (−0.6)
−6.9 (+0.4)	−8.8 (−1.8)	−6.5 (−0.3)	−6.2 (−0.6)	−7.5 (−0.9)
−1.6 (+3.1)**	−4.5 (−1.0)	−3.8 (+0.1)	−4.2 (+0.1)	−3.8 (+0.2)
−9.8 (−1.8)	−11.6 (−5.0)	−9.0 (−0.3)	−10.1 (−1.3)	−10.5 (−2.5)
6.4 (+2.1)	8.6 (+2.7)*	8.5 (+2.0)	4.2 (−3.2)	6.9 (+1.1)
−0.0 (−1.3)	−0.7 (−1.6)	−0.6 (+0.8)	−1.8 (−0.3)	−0.6 (−1.8)

Home Log Variables. Except for the *POMS* (Psychiatric Outpatient Mood Scale), home log variables are from daily responses in diaries kept by each subject. The *POMS* consists of an adjective checklist filled in weekly. Subjects were asked to consider their feeling for the entire week, not just that day.

Results

The results for amitriptyline compared to placebo are presented in Figures 2, 3, and 4 and in detail in Tables 1 and 2. There was some indication of an immediate hypnotic effect—a significant increase in total sleep time (Figure 2) and in Stage 2 and Stage 3 sleep time on early nights; time awake decreased in these normal subjects but not significantly. These changes were prominent only in the first 5 nights of administration, but total sleep remained somewhat elevated throughout administration. Slow-wave sleep (Stages 3 and 4) was somewhat but not significantly elevated throughout drug administration (Figure 3). D-time measured either as total D-time (Figure 4) or as percent D-time shows a clear decrease which continues throughout amitriptyline administration, and then a "rebound" increase lasting several days upon discontinuation. The above changes were even more pronounced when calculations were made for the first three hours of the night rather than for the whole night.

The subjective reports in the morning questionnaires show a slight but significant effect in the direction of feeling worse in the morning after amitriptyline, associated with increased scores on the "fatigue" scale of the POMS (Table 2).

An earlier study in our laboratory involving only a single night of administration showed effects similar to the early-night effects described above.[25]

There have been no controlled studies investigating specifically the effect of long-term amitriptyline administration on laboratory sleep patterns in depressed patients. However, one can draw tentative conclusions from records of individual patients who have taken part in sleep studies while under treatment with amitriptyline, and from results in depressed patients studied on a variety of antidepressant medications.[5,9,10,12] It appears that disturbed sleep, especially the sleep called pattern I above, improves on all its dimensions after amitriptyline and after other antidepressants. Laboratory studies of recovery of depressed patients under various treatment conditions suggest that almost all the parameters that show sleep disturbance—low Stage 4, increased waking, increased waking time, increased stage shifts—

return toward normal as the depression improves but that Stage 4 sleep may remain low for some time after improvement.[9]

Conclusions and Clinical Implications

Amitriptyline clearly has effects on sleep, noted clinically and demonstrated in sleep laboratory studies. There is an immediate effect, most prominent for 2 to 7 days, including drowsiness, increased total sleep, increase in Stages 2 and 3 sleep, and decreased D-time. Continued administration leads to return to near-normal levels for most variables, but a continued reduction in D-time. In depressed patients, amitriptyline treatment usually leads to improvement of the disturbances in sleep-waking patterns, concomitantly with improvement in the depression.

The clinical significance of the EEG changes demonstrated in normal subjects is so far uncertain. However, the fact that amitriptyline has an immediate hypnotic effect in addition to producing the longer term sleep changes found with other antidepressants suggests that it may be especially indicated in depressed patients with severely disturbed sleep (pattern I). In addition, there are some patients who complain of severe insomnia and show the sleep alterations of pattern I without other signs of overt depression; this may represent an aberrant or partial form of depression. Some patients with this syndrome have been successfully treated with amitriptyline, but it is too early to evaluate results definitively.

REFERENCES

1. Kleitman, N.: *Sleep and Wakefulness,* 2nd ed., Chicago, University of Chicago Press, 1963.

2. Dement, W. and Kleitman, N.: Cyclic variations in EEG during sleep and their relation to eye movements, body motility, and dreaming, Electroenceph. Clin. Neurophysiol. 9:673, 1957.

3. Hartmann, E.: *The Biology of Dreaming,* Springfield, Charles C Thomas, 1967.

4. Gresham, S. C., Agnew, H. W., Jr. and Williams, R. L.: The sleep of depressed patients, Arch. Gen. Psychiat. *13*:503, 1965.

5. Hartmann, E.: Longitudinal studies of sleep and dream patterns in manic-depressive patients, Arch. Gen. Psychiat. *19*:312, 1968.

6. Hauri, P. and Hawkins, D. R.: Individual differences in the sleep of depression. In *The Nature of Sleep,* ed. U. Jovanovic, Stuttgart, Gustav Fischer, 1973, pp. 193-197.

7. Hawkins, D. R., Mendels, J., Scott, J., Bensch, G. and Teachey, W.: The psychophysiology of sleep in psychotic depression: A longitudinal study, Psychosom. Med. *29*:329, 1967.

8. Kupfer, D. J., Foster, F. G. and Detre, T. P.: Sleep continuity changes in depression, Dis. Nerv. Syst. *34*:192, 1973.

9. Lowy, F. H., Cleghorn, J. M. and McClure, D. J.: Sleep patterns in depression: Longitudinal study of six patients and brief review of literature, J. Nerv. Ment. Dis. *153*:10, 1971.

10. Mendels, J. and Hawkins, D. R.: Sleep and depression: A controlled EEG study, Arch. Gen. Psychiat. *16*:344, 1967.

11. Mendels, J. and Hawkins, D. R.: Sleep and depression. IV. Longitudinal studies, J. Nerv. Ment. Dis. *153*:251, 1971.

12. Snyder, F.: Dynamic aspects of sleep disturbance in relation to mental illness, Biol. Psychiat. *1*:119, 1969.

13. Snyder, F.: Evolutionary theories of sleep: What, which, and whither? In *Perspectives in the Brain Sciences,* Vol. 1, *The Sleeping Brain,* ed. M. H. Chase, Los Angeles, BIS/Brain Research Institute, UCLA, 1972, pp. 40-43.

14. Zung, W. W., Wilson, W. P. and Dodson, W. E.: Effect of depressive disorders on sleep EEG responses, Arch. Gen. Psychiat. *10*:439, 1964.

15. Hartmann, E., Baekeland, F., Zwilling, G. and Hoy, P.: Sleep need: How much sleep and what kind?, Amer. J. Psychiat. *127*:1001, 1971.

16. Hartmann, E., Baekeland, F. and Zwilling, G. R.: Psychological differences between long and short sleepers, Arch. Gen. Psychiat. *26*:463, 1972.

17. Hartmann, E.: *The Functions of Sleep,* New Haven, Yale University Press, 1973, pp. 62-74.

18. Kupfer, D. J., Himmelhoch, J. M., Swartzburg, M., Anderson, C., Byck, R. and Detre, T. P.: Hypersomnia in manic-depressive disease (A preliminary report), Dis. Nerv. Syst. *33*:720, 1972.

19. Dobkin, A. B., Israel, J. S., Byles, P. H. and Lee, P. K. Y.: Chlorprothixene and amitriptyline: Interaction with thiopentone, circulatory effect and antisialogogue effect, Brit. J. Anaesth. *35*:425, 1963.

20. Allen, G. D. and Bonica, J. J.: Amitriptyline (Elavil) as an agent for premedication, Anesthesiology 26:571, 1965.

21. Urbach, K. E.: Hypnotic properties of amitriptyline: Comparison with secobarbital, Anesthesia and Analgesia: Current Researches 46:835, 1967.

22. Hartmann, E. and Cravens, J.: The effects of long term administration of psychotropic drugs on human sleep: I. Methodology and the effects of placebo, Psychopharmacologia 33:153, 1973.

23. Hartmann, E. and Cravens, J.: The effects of long term administration of psychotropic drugs on human sleep: III. The effects of amitriptyline, Psychopharmacologia 33:185, 1973.

24. Hartmann, E. and Cravens, J.: Long-term drug effects on human sleep. Presented to the First European Congress on Sleep Research, October, 1972. In *Sleep: Physiology, Biochemistry, Psychology, Pharmacology, Clinical Implications*, ed. W. P. Koella and P. Levin, Basel, S. Karger, 1973, pp. 477-485.

25. Hartmann, E.: The effect of four drugs on sleep patterns in man, Psychopharmacologia 12:346, 1968.

AMITRIPTYLINE IN THE MANAGEMENT OF DEPRESSION AND DEPRESSION ASSOCIATED WITH PHYSICAL ILLNESS

JOHN J. SCHWAB, M.D.
Professor of Psychiatry and Medicine
University of Louisville
School of Medicine
Louisville, Kentucky

John J. Schwab, M.D. is Professor and Chairman of the Department of Psychiatry at the University of Louisville School of Medicine and is Associate Editor of *Psychosomatics, Psychiatry in Medicine,* and *International Journal of Social Psychiatry.* He is also Co-Editor of *Social Psychiatry* (Annual Volume).

Dr. Schwab is Chairman of the Council on Research and Development, American Psychiatric Association, Liaison Officer of the American Psychiatric Association and the American Association for the Advancement of Science, and a Member of the National Institute of Mental Health Ad Hoc Committee, Collaborative Studies on the Epidemiology of Mental Illness. He holds membership in numerous professional and scientific societies and has authored or edited four books and scores of articles.

AMITRIPTYLINE
IN THE MANAGEMENT
OF DEPRESSION
AND
DEPRESSION ASSOCIATED
WITH PHYSICAL ILLNESS

INTRODUCTION

The recognition of depressive illness in general medical and surgical patients is critically important because physicians and surgeons have the first opportunity to diagnose and treat most patients with depression who eventually receive any type of care. The number of depressed persons requiring treatment is a public health problem of massive proportions. The National Institute of Mental Health (NIMH) recently estimated that eight million Americans are depressed,[1] that 125,000 are hospitalized each year for this condition, and that perhaps another 200,000 should be hospitalized. Some authorities believe that even these large figures are conservative; the prevalence of depression may be significantly greater than we realize, possibly involving 12 million adults. Furthermore, previous estimates indicated that anyone's chance of suffering from depressive illness serious enough to require treatment sometime in life was about 1 in 10.[2] Very possibly this chance is now as high as 1 in 7 or 8.

In his book, *Depressive Disorders in the Community,* written in 1966, C.A.H. Watts delineated "The Iceberg of Depression." His graphic portrayal showed that only about 18 per 1,000 persons in the general population are recognized as having depressions and that possibly at least as many as an additional 150 per 1,000 are "below the level of recognition" in that they never come to the attention of physicians. At the "tip of the iceberg" are the 0.12 per 1,000 suicides, and just below that the 2.8 per 1,000 who receive psychiatric care. Many more, 12 to 15 per 1,000, are treated by family practitioners.[3] More recently, Lehmann summarized the statistics, pointing out that only 1 out of 5 depressed persons receives medical treatment, that only 1 out of 50 is hospitalized, and that 1 in 200 commits suicide.[2]

With that epidemiologic picture as a background, this chapter will focus on the diagnosis and treatment of depression in medical practice. I will define depressive illness and sketch its varied symptomatology, present some of the types of depressions encountered by physicians, note the coexistence of depression and physical disease, and discuss the use of amitriptyline in treatment programs with these patients. Throughout the chapter I will emphasize problems in diagnosis and point out clues to the early recognition of depression, since physicians and surgeons, not psychiatrists, are the doctors who have the first opportunities to offer effective treatments which reduce human suffering and also may be life-saving.

DEFINITION AND SYMPTOMATOLOGY

To understand, diagnose, and treat depression in medical practice, we can conceptualize it as a multidimensional sociomedical syndrome. Its five major dimensions and the prominent symptomatology are:

(1) **Affective distress** typically expressed as lowered spirits and sadness but sometimes manifested by affective flattening which has a stolid or stoical quality, or by tense, grim smiles, pseudojocularity, or even mild degrees of hypomanic exhilaration.

(2) **A cognitive disorder** generally evidenced by self-disparagement and lowered self-esteem and often accompanied by veiled hostility which may be seen in more pronounced form when the patient verbalizes self-accusatory and self-punitive thoughts or suicidal ideation. At times, the cognitive disorder may have persecutory or slightly paranoidal overtones.

(3) **Psychobiologic disturbances** involving sleep, appetite and digestion, and sexuality. These disturbances appear in myriad changing forms and combinations. For example, the depressed patient may have trouble getting to sleep, repeated awakenings during the night, the more classical early morning awakening, or even hypersomnia. Generally, lack of refreshing sleep, regardless of its duration, and repeated complaints of fatigue in the morning as well as throughout the day are common. Analogously, the disturbances of appetite and digestion may range from anorexia to bulimia. The patient may complain that all food is tasteless, may describe new or particular likes and dislikes for various foods, or may tell that he is eating frequently and compulsively. Changes in bowel habits follow the dietary patterns. Constipation is a common symptom when the patient is eating poorly and when he is in the stage of psychomotor retardation. But the patient may have diarrhea or alternating bouts of diarrhea and constipation when he is indulging in food idiosyncrasies, drinking excessive coffee in order to relieve constant feelings of fatigue, or when he is taking or misusing medications.

Loss of interest in sexual activity and/or inability to reach an orgasm is a frequent complaint. But in the early stages of depression, women, and probably more often men, sometimes strive to become sexually more active as they consciously or unconsciously endeavor to compensate for self-perceived fears about loss of sexual attractiveness and sexual functions.

(4) **A host of somatic symptoms** usually consisting of persistent low-grade aches and pains in various parts of the body and an unrelieved sense of muscular tension which persists not only

throughout the day, but also at night during wakeful periods. Chronic headaches which neither increase in intensity nor disappear completely, occurring daily for weeks or months, are often the presenting and repeated complaints. Backaches and more vague, yet constant or repetitive, aches and pains in the extremities which resemble the symptoms of arthritis are other common bodily manifestations. Deep visceral aches and pains are not reported frequently by depressed patients although sometimes patients attempt to describe their inner sense of emptiness and hollowness as a "deep ache" in the chest or abdomen.

(5) **A philosophic dimension** usually characterized by a gloomy outlook on the future, a feeling that life is not worthwhile, and a personal sense of anguish and dread about human existence.

MASKED DEPRESSION

Not all patients will evidence symptoms indicative of all the various dimensions, especially in the early stages of depression—the critical time for diagnosis, when they are first seen by physicians and before the full-blown syndrome is so prominent that the need for psychiatric care is obvious. The medical patient who denies sadness or who does not manifest apathy or despair is often considered to have a "masked depression."[3,4] The popular concept, "masked depression," may be useful, but the clinician should recall that depression is a multidimensional sociomedical syndrome and the affective components represent only one of the dimensions. Affective symptoms may be withheld or disguised, particularly by male patients. When the physician questions the patient about psychosocial events, losses in his personal or family life, an inability to obtain gratification at home or at work, or lack of achievement, and obtains affirmative evidence of the presence of such problems and difficulties as well as a disturbance of psychobiologic activity, the tentative diagnosis of depression is justified. Of all the symptoms, those indicative of a psychobiologic disorder involving sleep, appetite and digestion, and sexuality are the most critical ones for establishing the diagnosis.

INTERPERSONAL AND
SOCIAL IMPLICATIONS

All of the dimensions of the depressive syndrome have interpersonal and larger social implications. For example, depressive mood can be contagious within the family setting; or a depressed husband's or wife's sadness, apathy, chronic complaints, or irritability may evoke hostility from other family members. Probably more often than we know, the apparently hypochondriacal wife who is haunting her doctor's office with numerous complaints may be reacting symptomatically to her husband's depressed state—the husband who is not seeking needed medical care for himself because his depression is serving as a barrier to his obtaining a diagnostic work-up. Importantly, although the psychobiologic disturbances and the somatic complaints with their hypochondriacal character may stimulate some patients to frequent physicians' offices, we should be ever mindful that depression may be an impediment to obtaining health care. A person may be so slowed down by the depression that he procrastinates about making an appointment to see his physician either for the symptoms of depression or for the symptoms of a coexisting physical disability. Even more gravely, the depressed person may engage in microsuicidal behavior by neglecting to seek medical care for physical complaints indicative, possibly, of a serious disease process.

At work, the depressed person's complaining, inability to concentrate, changed behavior, or drinking during the day for an "uplift" can be disruptive to the office routine. And some of the broader social implications of depression were revealed by one of our studies of depressive symptomatology and social change. We found that those persons in the general population who had high scores on a depression inventory were less aware of and less concerned about some of our social problems than were those with low depression scores.[5]

TYPES OF DEPRESSION

Diagnosing depression in medical practice hinges upon a constant awareness of the various dimensions of the depressive syndrome with its myriad symptomatology and upon an understanding of the types of depressive reactions. There is continuing controversy over the typology of depression. Perhaps the simplest, and a useful clinical classification, is the broad categorization into two major types, the endogenous and the reactive.[6,7] The distinctions between the two types are relative. Conventionally, the endogenous type is thought to be caused primarily by a biological disturbance. The patient often has a history of manic as well as depressive episodes or of sharp cyclothymic disturbances, and a family history of manic-depressive illness. The patient's depressive illness first appears early in adult life and recurs periodically, often with few objectively discernible precipitating environmental causes. The affective symptoms, and particularly the psychobiologic disorders, are generally pronounced. In contrast, the patient with a reactive depression can usually give a history of a precipitating factor—a loss that is real, threatened, or imaginary. The initial depressive episode may not appear until the person is in mid-life and the family history of depressive illness is not so obvious. The reactively depressed person's symptomatology may be more varied, diffuse, or obscure. Sometimes the affective components are not apparent since the patient may be suppressing sadness and emphasizing his somatic complaints.

Goodwin and Bunney state that the dichotomy, endogenous or reactive, may be misleading.[8] True, it may not be too helpful in research on the etiology of depressive illness, because it implies that one type, the endogenous, is biological while the other type, the reactive, is to a much greater extent environmentally produced by stressful events and circumstances, particularly losses. However, depression in medical practice is often a variable and an atypically manifested clinical condition, and the distinction—endogenous or reactive—has some utility for the physician. Psychiatric referral is more generally indicated for the medical patient with endogenous depression. When the patient is seen as reactively depressed, the physician is on surer grounds employing environmental therapies.

The classification of depressions as unipolar or bipolar is becoming popular.[8,9] Unipolar refers to manifestations of one type, exclusively depressive or, very rarely, exclusively hypomanic or manic, while bipolar refers to the oscillations and cycles of hypomania and depression. This classification is particularly useful when lithium is being contemplated for treatment since it is highly effective in both the treatment and prevention of hypomanic and manic illnesses.

With these exceptions, however, I think that depression in medical practice can be understood more comprehensively and more pragmatically when the doctor uses the categorization *endogenous* or *reactive*.

Moreover, the physician needs to view depression in medical practice from several overlapping frames of reference. These include an appreciation of: (1) the sociodemographic characteristics of the afflicted, particularly age, sex, and race relationships; and (2) the sequential and other relationships between depression and physical illnesses.

SOCIODEMOGRAPHIC RELATIONSHIPS

Depression in the Young

Conventionally, it has been thought that depression is more common in older than in younger-aged persons and that it has a very high frequency in females about the time of the menopause.[2] More recent studies, however, point to a high frequency of depression in adolescents and young adults, many of whom are using drugs for self-treatment, or are experiencing depression when they attempt to leave the drug culture, or are otherwise under-going withdrawal.[10,11] The rising suicide rate in the young evidences the seriousness of depression in this age group.[10,11,12] It portends possible epidemic depression since those who reacted early in life with depression will be susceptible to the development of depression later in life when they encounter loss, adversity, lack of satisfaction, and other stressful events and circumstances. Contrary to some widely held beliefs, many of these young people do seek medical assistance; in fact, they may frequent doctors' offices seeking help—not for their depression which they fear will not be understood by professionals, but often for seemingly minor complaints such as repeated bouts of pharyngitis, other ENT problems, minor infections, joint aches and pains, visual disturbances, etc. Requesting such a patient with an apparently minor ailment to return for a follow-up visit in a week or so will help the physician develop a relationship with the young person who then may begin to talk about feelings of futility and a sense of depression. At that time, the physician can begin anti-depressive treatment and, as indicated, refer the patient to counselors, the clergy, or others who are grappling with the many life-problems presented by young persons.

Depression in the Elderly

Other than the brain syndromes, depression is the most common psychiatric disorder of the elderly—the 20 million Americans over the age of 65. At least 3 million of the elderly need health services and another 1 million are institutionalized. Studies of geriatric patients show that about 40 percent of them are clinically depressed; their depressions are complicated by physical disabilities and by overlapping hypochondriacal concerns as well as by poverty, isolation, and loneliness. Sensory loss, evidenced by loss of hearing, which occurs in at least 30 percent of old people, and visual difficulties, which afflict at least 20 percent, contribute to the sense of isolation and powerlessness which abets depression.[13,14,15]

In our community study of 1,645 adults in the general population, we found that much higher percentages of the elderly than the other age groups reported the following symptoms "often or all the time": lowered spirits, feeling alone and helpless, feeling that life is hopeless, a gloomy outlook on the future, a sense of powerlessness, sleeping difficulties, loss of appetite, and periods when they could not take care of things. Such symptoms as crying spells and all sorts of bodily complaints were not expressed more frequently by the elderly, and self-blame was reported by a much smaller percentage of the elderly than by those in other age groups.[10]

Depression in Women

Numerous epidemiologic studies show that depression is somewhat more frequent among women than men. This is to be expected since women, in their restricted, often stressful roles as wives and mothers, tend more often than men to internalize rather than act out their distress when confronted with losses and sorrows.

Some of our studies of depression in the general population revealed that women in their late 40s, and particularly in their early 50s, were more likely than those in other age groups to evince depressive symptomatology.[16] The apparent age shift from the "traditional" menopausal syndrome of the mid-40s to the mid-50s may be attributed to biological factors such as better nutrition, increased use of female hormones, etc., as well as to changing family structures. Often, the last child leaves home when the woman is aged 50 to 55 and then the "empty nest syndrome" appears.[17] The woman in her early 50s, therefore, is frequently confronted with the necessity to change roles (for which she may be quite unprepared) and to adopt new attitudes and activities. In medical practice, these women often present with complaints resembling hypothyroidism or metabolic disorders such as hypoglycemia. The differential diagnosis is a critical one; these patients should be evaluated by tests for endocrine and metabolic disturbances, but the clinician also should be aware that psychic distress and endocrine malfunction are intimately related and that a "both-and" rather than an "either-or" approach is required to insure comprehensive treatment.

Depression in Blacks

Depression is now being diagnosed much more frequently in blacks than in the past.[16] Yet, many black patients have unrecognized depressions. The white physician often has difficulty evaluating his black patient's affect for a number of reasons. One is social distance—the gap between the races that inhibits the perception of feelings. Another is the black medical patient's sense that his feelings cannot possibly be understood by white middle-class doctors and nurses who know little or nothing, at firsthand, about what it means to belong to a minority group with its particular dilemmas and different cultural modes of expression. But epidemiologic evidence, particularly the rising suicide rate among blacks, points to the growing seriousness of the problem of their unrecognized and untreated depressive illnesses.[12]

Several symptoms are particularly valuable indicators of depression in blacks. Especially the complaint of headache—low-grade and persistent, that is never completely relieved by analgesics and that seldom increases sharply in intensity—may be a signal of depression. Comparable complaints of backache, aches and pains in the extremities, and fatigue are also major diagnostic clues to the possibility of depression in black medical patients. In such instances, the physician is justified in launching a vigorous treatment program for depression on a trial basis, for at least a month, after he has carried out a thorough medical work-up.

Depression in Low Income Groups

The last of the major sociodemographic relationships with depression is low income. In our studies, depressive symptomatology was reported significantly more often by patients from the lower socioeconomic strata than by the more affluent.[16,18] The frequency of the symptoms of futility, apathy, and despair, coupled with sleep disturbances, and the increased prevalence of physical illnesses describe a haunting, poignant configuration of human misery. Moreover, it is difficult to distinguish between the symptoms of depression and the manifestations of poverty. The physician is confronted with the questions: Is this social or medical distress? Or both? What can I do? And, the physician may be overwhelmed by his own inner feelings of identification and helplessness: If I lived with all of those problems wouldn't I, too, be depressed? But when the poor and deprived are given adequate medical treatment, then they are sometimes able to better their life circumstances. And therapeutic trials with antidepressants should be administered frequently when depression, per se, is an additional obstacle blocking the poverty-stricken patient's efforts to improve his living conditions.

MEDICAL RELATIONSHIPS

Depression as Foreshadowing

Understanding the sequential relationships between depression and medical and surgical illness is critically important. Depression precedes, accompanies, simulates, or follows medical and surgical conditions. Much more often than we generally realize, patients who require care for serious illnesses, such as coronary heart disease or malignancies, have been depressed for weeks or months before defined physical disease is apparent. Some of these patients have experienced object loss prior to the onset of their physical illnesses. Schmale and his coworkers at Rochester view object loss as a predisposing event which alters the organism's reactivity and increases its vulnerability to disease processes.[19]

Clinical experience has taught us that especially males in their 50s and 60s who present with depressive symptomatology should be carefully and thoroughly evaluated for early malignancies. In 1931, Yaskin wrote about nervous symptoms, particularly those of depression, as the *earliest* manifestations of carcinoma of the pancreas.[20] In 1967, this was confirmed by Fras and his co-workers at Mayo Clinic who found that depressive symptoms were often the first indicators of pancreatic and retroperitoneal neoplasms.[21]

Depression as a Concomitant

The coexistence of depression and physical illness is a common phenomenon. We have found that medical patients with gastrointestinal diseases are likely to be suffering from concurrent depressions which require treatment.[22,23] The possibility that gastrointestinal disease disposes the patient to depression cannot be ruled out. Dewhurst has indicated that gastrointestinal dysfunction may interfere with the absorption and metabolism of the precursors of the catecholamines, resulting in possible insufficiency.[24] Furthermore, the high frequency of concurrent depression and gastrointestinal disorders substantiates certain elements of psychoanalytic theory regarding fixation in the oral and anal stages of development as providing the psychosexual background for depression and also the "choice" of the gastrointestinal tract as the illness site.

Depression as a Cause

Depression simulating physical illness, particularly the unresolved grief reaction or the anniversary reaction, is a condition which, too often, is not identified by physicians and surgeons.

Case History #1

A typical case history is that of a 42-year-old minister's wife who had been observed and treated symptomatically by her family doctor for 18 months for attacks of "indigestion and possible gall bladder disease." Because her complaints recurred, and because diagnostic studies of biliary tract function were not absolutely normal, she was referred to the Medical Center for a complete diagnostic evaluation. Physical examination showed little more than moderate obesity and thorough gastrointestinal studies revealed only that her gall bladder probably emptied "sluggishly." On the medical inpatient unit, the interns, and particularly the nurses, reported that she was alternately apathetic and helpless or whining and demanding. After ten days, she was referred for psychiatric consultation. The psychiatrist found that she was guarded, tense, and somewhat fearful of discussing personal matters, especially those referable to her husband. But when the psychiatrist learned from her family history that her mother had died from carcinoma of the stomach about two years before, and when he asked about her grief reaction, she told that she and her husband had been in charge of the funeral arrangements and that they had taken care of the numerous relatives who had attended the funeral. Moreover, her husband had forbidden her to show her own feelings of loss since "he and she were supposed to set an example for the members of the community; after all, in his work he customarily participated in funeral ceremonies and her job was to comfort the bereaved." When the psychiatrist probed her feelings she broke into tears, mentioned marital problems, and discussed the many demands placed upon her and her husband. Treatment with moderate dosage of amitriptyline and two follow-up visits at monthly intervals produced improvement. About six months later, her family doctor reported that she was vastly improved.

Case History #2

Another brief case vignette concerns a 50-year-old, small-business man whose semiannual or annual attacks of chest pain, severe enough to require observation in the hospital for three to four days each time, had been recurring for five years. Finally, in the Medical Center, the medical resident learned that the patient's father, who had founded the small family business, had died of a myocardial infarction seven years before. Careful history-taking, in the light of the history of the father's death, showed that the patient became ill either on the anniversary of the father's death or at times when he made business decisions which he feared might be counter to what his father would have done. In this instance, the patient was not given antidepressant medications; instead, he and his personal physician were informed of the timing of the attacks and of the repressed feelings and fears. The physician agreed to see the patient for brief psychotherapy—as a counselor and friend—at periodic intervals and, as a result, the attacks of chest pain and "possible heart attacks" subsided.

Depression in Convalescence

Depression commonly follows infectious diseases such as infectious hepatitis and viral pneumonia. Particularly during convalescence, these patients exhibit depressive symptomatology. In fact, those with the lassitude, malaise, and irritability of the posthepatitic syndrome, and those with marked fatigue and lethargy following viral pneumonia should be given therapeutic trials with antidepressants such as amitriptyline when depression is diagnosed.

Large numbers of patients with cardiovascular diseases become depressed. During the convalescent stage, one to two months after sustaining a myocardial infarction, many patients develop full-blown depressive reactions when their initial anxiety has subsided and they realize the gravity of their illness and the need for changing their patterns of living. In other patients, those with cerebral vascular disease, reduced mobility leads to a life of dependency, isolation, and loneliness that is conducive to depression. Tricyclic antidepressants, including amitriptyline, are not recommended during the acute recovery phase following myocardial infarction. Moreover, patients with cardiovascular disorders should be monitored closely while on these drugs.

THE USE OF AMITRIPTYLINE IN MEDICAL PRACTICE

Outpatients

With certain exceptions, amitriptyline is a highly useful antidepressant medication for depressed medical patients. In some of these patients, the diagnosis of depression can be made easily. Diagnostic accuracy is increased by knowing that the frequency of depression is high among these patients, awareness of the symptomatology, and sensitivity to both the patient's despondency and to the doctor's own feelings which the patient contact has engendered. These feelings of the doctor, developing as he works with depressed medical patients, may include sadness, futility, exasperation, and/or a sense of anger.

Depression also should be suspected in certain groups of medical outpatients. These include: (1) the numerous patients who complain of chronic low-grade aches and pains in various parts of the body; (2) those with gastrointestinal symptomatology who may or may not have demonstrable physical lesions; and (3) all who report disturbances of appetite, sexual activity, and, especially, sleep.

Treatment Regimen

When depression is diagnosed for adult outpatients, I usually begin treatment with amitriptyline, 10 mg t.i.d. and 50 mg h.s. Generally, I recommend that the patient begin taking the medication at a time when he or she can stay away from work for one or two days, free from the demands of the daily routine, and when it is possible to obtain extra sleep since amitriptyline may impair mental or physical abilities required in the performance of hazardous tasks. Depending upon the patient's responsivity to the medication, I change the dosage to 25 mg t.i.d., and continue 50 mg h.s.

Alternative Approach

An alternative procedure is to administer a single daily dosage of 50 to 100 mg at bedtime for a few days and then increase it to 100 to 150 mg. These dosages should be used only for the average-sized adult outpatient in the age range of 25 to 60 years, whose general physical condition is fairly good. Adolescents should almost always be started on low dosages, 10 mg t.i.d., and 20 mg h.s., until their reactions to the medication can be evaluated, since they often tend to report excessive drowsiness even on small daily dosages. At the other end of the age span, among elderly patients, I always begin treatment with a small dosage, 10 mg two or three times per day, and 20 mg h.s.

The conservative, small dosage which I have outlined for medical outpatients should be increased as necessary, recognizing that an adequate therapeutic response may take as long as 30 days to develop. Some of these patients may require a total daily dosage of 150 mg since a therapeutic response may not be obtained when the daily dosage is maintained at a lower level.

Two case vignettes illustrate the use of amitriptyline with medical outpatients:

Case History #3

A 53-year-old black male was seen in psychiatric consultation in the medical clinic because of continued complaints of headache, backache, and weakness which had started six months previously. At that time, a large refrigerator that he was unloading slipped from the dolly; he fell to the side and narrowly escaped being crushed. During the next few weeks, he complained of nervousness at work and aches and pains from the minor bruises he sustained. Then he stopped working because of headache, backache, and weakness, for which no physical basis could be found and which did not respond to treatment with analgesics. Psychiatric evaluation revealed that he was tense and sad, and, upon questioning, he told that he was sleeping poorly and was unable to eat well. He was started on amitriptyline 25 mg t.i.d. and then 50 mg h.s., and was seen for brief follow-up visits in the clinic at weekly intervals. At the end of the first week, he told that he was eating and sleeping much better than he had for months; and at the end of three weeks he felt so much better that he was able to return to work. He was continued on the same dosage of amitriptyline for two months; the daily dosage was reduced during the next month to 50 mg h.s. and then discontinued. From a psychiatric point of view, this patient probably suffered from a traumatic neurosis which was superseded by depression.

Case History #4

A second case was that of a 27-year-old medical student's wife who requested a complete medical work-up because of general nervousness and overeating. She feared that she had a thyroid disturbance because she had a family history of goiter and of hypothyroidism, and in her work as a secretary to a physician she had become familiar with the symptoms of myxedema. A complete diagnostic evaluation revealed no evidence of a physical disorder. The internist sensed that she was emotionally disturbed and referred her for psychiatric consultation. She related that she had been "worried and depressed" for about three months since her husband had started his clinical clerkships. She thought that he was staying at the hospital for unnecessarily long periods of time at night, and finally told that she feared that he was having an affair with a nurse. Night after night she watched television, snacked, and waited anxiously for his return. Their sexual activity diminished drastically, adding to her fears about his possible infidelity and increasing her concern about her unattractiveness which she attributed to her 20-pound weight gain. She was started on amitriptyline, 10 mg t.i.d., 50 mg h.s., for a few days while she continued to work. On the weekend the dosage was raised to 25 mg t.i.d. and 50 mg h.s., and continued. During weekly, 30-minute psychotherapy sessions, she was urged to increase her contacts with other medical students' wives and also to develop a more active social life for her and her husband with other students. At the end of one month she was greatly improved; she exhibited greater vivacity and told that she had begun to diet. She was seen briefly for follow-up sessions at monthly intervals for the next three months, at which time she was so greatly improved that the medication was discontinued gradually over a two-week period.

Inpatients

For hospitalized adult patients, I generally prescribe divided daily doses of 25 mg and 50 mg h.s. (approximately 100 mg).

This can be increased gradually to 200 mg a day if necessary. As for outpatients, the elderly person should be started on a smaller dosage, 10 mg t.i.d. and 20 mg h.s. for the first two to three days. But then, the total daily dose should be raised if necessary to 100 to 150 mg.

Many depressed medical patients respond therapeutically to amitriptyline, particularly when the physician utilizes a psychotherapeutic approach. This involves exploring losses—real or symbolic—and helping the patient identify and express his feelings. Such feelings usually consist primarily of sadness, emptiness, and helplessness, but are often admixed with bitterness and anger. A comprehensive treatment program also includes the development or reinforcement of the patient's social support system. This involves urging the patient to initiate contacts with family, neighbors, the church, etc., and also calling upon the assistance of allied mental health professional and lay groups.

Some depressed medical patients do not seem to be responding to amitriptyline. Often, these are patients who are receiving an insufficient daily dosage. Raising the daily dosage to 125 to 150 mg is often therapeutic. But, in some instances, when the doctor is fearful of an adverse reaction or when the patient complains of excessive side effects, hospitalizing him for about a week and raising the daily dosage to the maximal limit is the preferred approach. Some other depressed medical patients who do not respond to amitriptyline should be referred for psychiatric evaluation and, possibly, intensive psychiatric treatments.

How Long to Treat

Many medical patients require maintenance therapy. In our consultation work we have found repeatedly that physicians tend to reduce the therapeutic dosage, 75 to 150 mg per day, as soon as the patient reports that his symptoms are being alleviated. Too often, these patients' depressive symptoms reappear in a chronic, low-grade form which would have been prevented by adequate maintenance therapy over a six- to nine-month period with a gradual reduction in dosage over a two- to four-week period until the medication is discontinued.

Many depressed medical patients will report some improvement within five to ten days after treatment with amitriptyline has been started. In addition to the drug's antidepressant action, this initial improvement is probably produced by a number of other factors, including a discussion of the possibility of depression, the concomitant identification and expression of feelings, and improved sleep due to the sedative effect of the drug. In a recent study, Klerman and his associates noted that over 70 percent of 278 neurotic depressed patients (most depressed patients in medical practice have neurotic depressions) showed "a significant clinical improvement within four to six weeks after amitriptyline therapy was initiated" in therapeutic dosage.[25]

Therapeutic Trial: Problems and Opportunities

In this chapter, I have mentioned a number of times that physicians are justified in using amitriptyline for a therapeutic trial in depressed patients. In such instances, after a test dose and over a three- to four-day period, the patient should be given 100 to 150 mg per day for at least four weeks to evaluate the medication's usefulness. Smaller dosage over a shorter period of time does not constitute an adequate therapeutic trial.

In all instances, the physician should be aware of the contraindications, warnings, and precautions related to the use of amitriptyline as well as its possible adverse reactions. In medical practice, the medication's possible blocking of the antihypertensive action of guanethidine or similarly acting compounds should be noted and the patient taking such antihypertensives should be carefully monitored. Because of its atropine-like action, amitriptyline should be used with caution in patients with increased intraocular pressure, urinary retention, or a history of angle-closure glaucoma. Occasional paradoxical reactions do occur; these are manifested usually by confusion, agitation, and even disturbances of perception. Also, hypomanic or manic-type episodes may result. Generally, these undesirable effects are seen within a few days after the medication is first prescribed; treatment consists of promptly discontinuing the drug and administering sedatives. The drug should not be given to those who have received an MAOI within two weeks.

In medical practice, one of the greatest problems concerns the possible use of antidepressants for patients who are depressed and who have recently sustained a myocardial infarction. Often, one is confronted by a dilemma in such cases: the depression may be so severe that it is adversely influencing the medical care and recovery, and, simultaneously, the antidepressant may have a deleterious effect on the cardiovascular system. At such times it is best to provide optimal supporting care and small doses of a minor tranquilizer since amitriptyline is contraindicated in view of its possible adverse effects on the cardiovascular system. The more usual side effects of amitriptyline, e.g., dryness of the mouth and/or excessive drowsiness during the first few days after it has been started, seldom necessitate discontinuance of the medication in medical patients. When informed of the possible anticholinergic effects of the medication, patients usually accept the unpleasantness and minor annoyances. Furthermore, almost all depressed patients have been sleeping poorly for a number of weeks or months; therefore, I generally advise them during the first week after amitriptyline therapy has been initiated not to struggle against drowsiness but, instead, to catch up on lost sleep. Of course, in all such circumstances, the patient is advised not to engage in tasks or be placed in situations which require intellectual precision and alertness.

SUMMARY

In summary, depression is a serious public health problem. Physicians and surgeons, not psychiatrists, have the first opportunities to identify and treat these patients since depression precedes, coexists with, simulates, and/or follows physical disabilities for which patients seek medical care. Furthermore, depressive symptomatology appears in myriad changing forms. Alertness to the relationships with physical disease and an appreciation of the multidimensional quality of depression enable doctors to institute therapies which reduce human suffering and may be life-saving since suicide is the fatal outcome for some depressed patients. Amitriptyline is a useful antidepressant which has a significant place in the number of medications which are available to the doctor. Like all medications, it is most effective when the doctor-patient relationship is characterized by trust, empathy, and humanistic concerns.

REFERENCES

1. Elkind, D. and Hamsher, J.: The anatomy of melancholy, Sat. Rev. 55(40):54, 1972.

2. Lehmann, H.E.: Epidemiology of depressive disorders. In *Depression in the 70's*, ed. R.R. Fieve, The Netherlands, Excerpta Medica, 1971, pp. 21-30.

3. Parry-Jones, W.L.: "Masked" depressive illness, Update Int. 1(4):239, 1974.

4. Dorfman, W.: Recognition and management of masked depression in clinical practice, N.Y. State J. of Med. 74(2):373, 1974.

5. Schwab, J.J.: Perception of social change and depressive symptomatology. In *Social Psychiatry*, Vol. I, ed. J.H. Masserman and J.J. Schwab, New York, Grune & Stratton. In press.

6. Kiloh, L.G. and Garside, R.F.: The independence of neurotic depression and endogenous depression, Brit. J. Psychiat. 109:451, 1963.

7. Beck, A.T.: *Depression: Clinical, Experimental and Theoretical Aspects*, New York, Evanston, and London; Hoeber Medical Division, Harper & Row, 1967, pp. 60-74.

8. Goodwin, F.K. and Bunney, W.E., Jr.: A psychobiological approach to affective illness, Psychiat. Ann. 3(2):19, 1973.

9. Winokur, G.: Diagnostic and genetic aspects of affective illness, Psychiat. Ann. 3(2):7, 1973.

10. Schwab, J.J., Holzer, C.E., III and Warheit, G.J.: Depressive symptomatology and age, Psychosom. 14(3):135, 1973.

11. Cherry, R. and Cherry, L.: The common cold of mental ailments—Depression, The N.Y. Times Mag., Nov. 25, 1973, p. 38.

12. Suicide in California, Resident and Staff Physician *19(10)*:58, 1973.

13. Butler, R.N. and Lewis, M.I.: *Aging and Mental Health: Positive Psychosocial Approaches,* St. Louis, The C.V. Mosby Company, 1973, pp. 5-33, 50-60, and 247-248.

14. Pfeiffer, E. and Busse, E.W.: Mental disorders in later life—Affective disorders; paranoid, neurotic, and situational reactions. In *Mental Illness in Later Life,* ed. E.W. Busse and E. Pfeiffer, Washington, D.C., American Psychiatric Association, 1973, pp. 116-141.

15. Schwab, J.J.: Depression among the aged. Presented at the 55th Annual Session of The American College of Physicians, New York City, April 1-4, 1974. To be published.

16. Warheit, G.J., Holzer, C.E., III and Schwab, J.J.: An analysis of social class and racial differences in depressive symptomatology: A community study, J. of Health and Soc. Beh. *14(4)*:291, 1973.

17. Deykin, E., Jacobson, S., Klerman, G. and Solomon, M.: The empty nest: Psychosocial aspects of conflict between depressed women and their grown children, Amer. J. Psychiat. *122(12)*:1422, 1966.

18. Schwab, J.J., Holzer, C.E., III, Warheit, G.J. and Schwab, R.B.: Human ecology and symptoms of depression. Presented at the Colloquium on the Range of Normality, Cincinnati, Ohio, October 19-21, 1973. In *Social Psychiatry*, Vol. II, ed. J.H. Masserman and J.J. Schwab, New York, Grune & Stratton. In preparation.

19. Schmale, A.H., Jr., Meyerowitz, S. and Tinling, D.C.: Current concepts of psychosomatic medicine. In *Modern Trends in Psychosomatic Medicine—2,* ed. O.W. Hill, New York, Appleton-Century-Crofts; London, Butterworths, 1970, pp. 1-25.

20. Yaskin, J.C.: Nervous symptoms as earliest manifestations of carcinoma of the pancreas, JAMA *96*:1664, 1931.

21. Fras, I., Litin, E.M. and Pearson, J.S.: Comparison of psychiatric symptoms in carcinoma of the pancreas with those in some other intra-abdominal neoplasms, Amer. J. Psychiat. *123(12)*:1553, 1967.

22. Schwab, J.J., Bialow, M., Brown, J.M. and Holzer, C.E.: Diagnosing depression in medical inpatients, Ann. of Int. Med. *67(4)*:695, 1967.

23. Schwab, J.J., Brown, J.M. and Holzer, C.E.: Depression in medical inpatients with gastrointestinal diseases, Amer. J. Gastroenterol. *49(2)*:146, 1968.

24. Dewhurst, W.G.: On the chemical basis of mood, J. Psychosom. Res. *9*:115, 1965.

25. Klerman, G.L., Dimascio, A., Weissman, M., Prusoff, B. and Paykel, E.S.: Treatment of depression by drugs and psychotherapy, Amer. J. Psychiat. *131(2)*:186, 1974.

5

AMITRIPTYLINE IN THE MANAGEMENT OF THE ELDERLY DEPRESSED PATIENT

ALVIN I. GOLDFARB, M.D.
Associate Clinical Professor of Psychiatry
The Mount Sinai School of Medicine
The City University of New York
New York, New York

Alvin I. Goldfarb, M.D. is Associate Clinical Professor of Psychiatry, Mount Sinai School of Medicine of the City University of New York, and Adjunct Clinical Professor of Psychiatry, New York Medical College. He is also Associate Attending Psychiatrist in Charge of Geriatric Services at Mount Sinai Hospital and Consultant Neuropsychiatrist, Jewish Home and Hospital for the Aged, both in New York City.

Dr. Goldfarb is past Chairman of both the Task Force on Aging and the Committee on Aging, American Psychiatric Association, was Chairman of the Committee on Aging, Group for Advancement of Psychiatry, and Chairman of the Clinical Medicine Section, The Gerontological Society (1973-74). In addition, he is a Fellow of the American Academy of Neurology, the American Psychiatric Association, the American College of Psychiatry, the American College of Psychoanalysts, and a member of the American Psychoanalytic Association. He is currently President of the Group for Geriatric Psychiatry of New York.

AMITRIPTYLINE IN THE MANAGEMENT OF THE ELDERLY DEPRESSED PATIENT

INTRODUCTION

Amitriptyline is useful in the treatment of clinically significant depression in the elderly and aged. The drug is most effective in the episodic depressive disorders carried into old age that first emerged in youth or middle life, but is also helpful in the depressive reactions that develop or first emerge as important in old age.

Proper treatment of depressed older persons can greatly ease problems of management and add to the quality of their lives. In the etiology of mental disorders of old people, there is a tendency to overestimate the importance of brain dysfunction and brain damage which is reflected by organic brain syndromes. This leads to the incorrect labelling of many old persons as "senile" or as having "cerebral arteriosclerosis" and consequently leads to pessimism about the value and outcome of treatment. This incorrect labelling may lead to relative neglect or incorrect treatment.

This chapter will briefly discuss the use of amitriptyline in the most common depressive disorders of late life.

SPECIAL PROBLEMS OF THE OLD

In the chronologically old and aged, depressive disorders are frequently complicated by physical changes. Depression in the aged may be complicated by losses of physical, social, and economic resources, as well as by intellectual deficit on the basis of brain dysfunction or brain damage. In all depressive states there is usually an interweaving of the physical, social, and economic factors of the present, together with the effects of the past and the personal expectations of the future.

Physical impairment: Sensory impairment of all kinds—visual, auditory, equilibratory, taste, and smell—are common in old age. With all physical impairment there is an interweaving of somatic and psychological factors which often determines the exacerbation, exaggeration, aggravation, and exploitation of physical illness and the degree of disability. It may be difficult to measure how much disability is the direct result of physical impairment and how much is related to emotional causes. Aging individuals may react to illness or debility with feelings of helplessness and fear which are expressed as depression. Progressive cardiovascular disease, for example, with its recognized threat to life and its functional limitations, usually provokes fear, anger, and depressive reactions. At times, depression may mask the physical problems which contributed to its emergence. Depression frequently precedes and heralds the existence of a somatic disorder either because it accentuates the signs and symptoms and reveals the presence of the organic problem, or because it is itself a symptom of the underlying disorder and the limitation of activity caused by the physical problem.

Socioeconomic losses: The loss of family or friends, social position, money, residence, or occupation usually has adverse psychological effects. However, old persons who were poor in youth but who have achieved a measure of economic security because of social security or old age assistance may be less anxious, angry, or depressed than persons who, although richer, are largely dependent on relatives and an uncertain income. Financially secure persons appear to have higher morale than poor persons. In general, from the point of view of morale, it seems that it is better to be rich though sick, than poor and healthy.

In sum, while physical, psychological, and socioeconomic losses and changes may be important contributory factors in the emergence of depressive reactions in the aged, genetic factors, cultural factors, and life experiences prior to old age appear to be necessary for the emergence or development of typical depressive states in late life.

SOLVING DIAGNOSTIC PROBLEMS

Definitions

"Chronologically old" vs "aged": By *old, chronologically old,* or *elderly* is meant the age of 65 and over. By the *aged* is meant those in whom a measurable decline of physical or mental functional capacity is present which interferes with the performance of routine everyday tasks. The greater the chronological age of the person, the more likely there is to be such functional decline, although many very old persons do retain the functional capacities of youth. Physical impairment and mental impairment (organic brain syndrome) may limit the goals of the physician. It is important to recognize that disability often exceeds the amount expected from the actual physical impairment. Where this is true, the "excess disability" may be caused not only by organic brain syndrome (OBS) but also by an emotional disorder.

Organic brain syndrome: Organic brain syndrome is the psychiatric syndrome believed to reflect brain damage or dysfunction. The syndrome consists of disorientation (confusion), memory loss (both recent and remote), and defects of calculation and in the recall of simple information. *Organic brain syndrome, acute* is the term used to denote brain syndrome of the reversible type; it is the reflection of brain cell dysfunction. This reversible state may complicate depression and it may be the result of illness or drugs which reduce cerebral support or which have special central nervous system intoxicating effects. *Organic brain syndrome, chronic* is the term used to denote the presence of the same signs when they reflect brain cell loss—brain damage; here, the cognitive defects are irreversible.

Distinguishing Organic Brain Syndrome from Depression

Depression in the aged is commonly misdiagnosed as "senility" or organic brain syndrome (OBS). It is true that the older the person becomes, the greater the likelihood that brain damage and its psychiatric reflection (OBS) is present. However, even when OBS *is* present the patient may be depressed. Psychomotor retardation and apathy, or the converse, agitation and restlessness, should not be dismissed as senility. Depression is more often the cause.

Depression that develops or emerges as significant in old age can be subdivided into two major groups:

1. Depressive disorders in the absence of organic brain syndrome, and

2. Depressive disorders in the presence of organic brain syndrome, usually of mild to moderate degree.

Chronic OBS (which is a frequent sign of aging) may be present in mild to moderate degree in depressed old persons. The mood, content of thought, and overt behavior may be quite responsive to treatment despite the irreversibility of the intellectual deficit.

When OBS is severe, true depressive episodes are unusual: it seems to "take brains" to elaborate a depressive disorder. Nevertheless, there may be present a depression which can be relieved to some degree. Milder OBS may appear to be more severe than it is for emotional reasons—the patient may be depressed.

Since depression may mimic severe OBS, such treatable disorders might easily be neglected. Conversely, OBS may be misdiagnosed as depression and be exaggerated by drugs or electroconvulsive therapy (ECT). The use of simple rapid screening procedures such as the Mental Status Questionnaire and the Double Simultaneous Stimulation of the face and hand is advocated as an aid to differential diagnosis for correct treatment (see Tables 1, 2, 3). These special tests are simple and dependable tools for evaluating cognitive functioning.

Table 1. Mental status questionnaire—"Special 10"*

Question	Presumed test area
1. Where are we now?	Place
2. Where is this place (located)?	Place
3. What is today's date-day of month?	Time
4. What month is it?	Time
5. What year is it?	Time
6. How old are you?	Memory—recent or remote
7. What is your birthday?	Memory—recent or remote
8. What year were you born?	Memory—remote
9. Who is president of the U.S.?	General information—memory
10. Who was president before him?	General information—memory

Table 2. Rating of mental functional impairment by mental status questionnaire*

No. of errors	Presumed mental status
0-2	Chronic brain syndrome absent or mild
3-8	Chronic brain syndrome moderate
9-10	Chronic brain syndrome severe
Nontestable	Chronic brain syndrome severe†

†In the not uncooperative person without deafness or insuperable language barrier.

Table 3. Order of stimulation used in face-hand test*

Stimulation	Notes
1. Right cheek—left hand 2. Left cheek—right hand 3. Right cheek—right hand 4. Left cheek—left hand	Initial trials. Response evaluated in context of further trials.
5. Right cheek—left cheek 6. Right hand—left hand	Teaching trials. Almost always correctly reported. Examiner informs, or reinforces response that there were two touches.
7. Right cheek—left hand 8. Left cheek—right hand 9. Right cheek—right hand 10. Left cheek—left hand	Incorrect response and stimulation not reported, felt but displaced, projected or located in space is presumptive of brain damage.

*Tables 1 and 2 are reproduced by permission from Goldfarb, A. I.: The Evaluation of Geriatric Patients Following Treatment. In: *Evaluation of Psychiatric Treatment,* Hoch, P. H. and Zubin, J., editors. New York, Grune and Stratton, 1964, pp. 271-308. Table 3 is modified from Goldfarb, A. I., *ibid.*

Mental Status Questionnaire

The MSQ (Tables 1 and 2) may be used with elderly patients who are blind, bedridden, incontinent, disoriented, physically handicapped, and easily fatigued. Less mental impairment may be revealed by the MSQ in persons whose extensive education or occupational and social background provides them with well-developed habits of remaining oriented for time and place. Some patients may also answer incorrectly because of misinterpretation due to deafness. These patients could either use the stethoscope as an "ear trumpet," or, for those whose deafness is more a neuroperceptual matter, the physician can simply speak more slowly. But the MSQ can do more than measure the degree of brain syndrome. It can also provide information about behavioral patterns such as evasion, defensiveness, and hostility. These patterns are discernible in the patient's responses to MSQ questions asked either as a formal test or in general conversation.

Face-Hand Test

The face-hand test (Table 3) is conducted with the patient seated, facing the examiner, feet flat on the floor, hands resting on the knees. The examiner will touch or brush the patient simultaneously on one cheek and the dorsum of one hand, usually in the specified order. During the first series of 10, the patient's eyes should be closed, then the series is repeated with eyes open. A patient who learns to report correctly where he is touched after the trials 5 and 6 is presumed free of brain damage. Only errors on steps 7 to 10 are considered evidence of brain damage.

Recognizing the Depressive Disorders

Because of the difference in course and response to treatment, it is useful to divide the depressive disorders of the chronologically old into two major categories:

"Mood-cyclic disorders" and recurrent depressions: These recurrent illnesses (also known as manic-depressive psychoses) are common and appear to be genetically determined. Their intensity, the age at which they first emerge, how they are elaborated in thought and action, and even their periodicity, may be greatly influenced by "nurture." That is, they are influenced by the individual's cultural background, education, occupation, and the multiple modifying or reinforcing social factors of the lifetime which interact to determine the life-style or way of life. In these patients, the depressive state tends to occur with relative regularity and the episodes are limited, usually of predictable length, and are accompanied by somatic changes referable to the autonomic nervous system. There is prominent evidence of disturbances in gastrointestinal functions (e.g., anorexia or bulimia, constipation or diarrhea) and sleep (early morning waking), in addition to overt abnormal behavior; psychomotor retardation or agitation is commonly present, as well as inertia and decreased attention and concentration. Even in very old persons, the episodes tend to come to an end if the patient lives long enough and if there are no disturbing perpetuating complications. Generally, the course is predictable; however, the symptoms and signs of depression may fluctuate in their intensity and have a grossly impairing effect upon behavior and efficiency which differs from one episode to another.

"Depressive reactions" and psychoneurotic depressions: This large and varied group of disorders is usually characterized by seemingly psychological etiologic factors rather than genetic. It is likely that many depressive reactions have a strong genetically determined core. From a psychotherapeutic viewpoint, however, they can usually be regarded as signals of distress to the environment (based upon complex psychodynamic factors). The "psychoneurotic" disorders are those which appear to be more clearly the result of the interaction of forces in the early life period. Although intense, often recurrent, and usually accompanied by somatic concomitants of strong emotion, the *depressive reaction**

---

*This term is often mistakenly noted as "reactive depression" which carries the erroneous connotation that the depression is a *reaction to* something (environment, problems, etc.). A *depressive reaction* is a particular kind of psychological syndrome, but not necessarily *as a result* of any identifiable event or situation.

95

and the psychoneurotic depression are not as clearly episodic or so well defined in course as the attacks of mood change in the mood cyclic disorder. The depressive reaction and psychoneurotic depressions are each more clearly recognizable as a motivated "search for aid." Subjective distress is often the chief complaint and anxiety is commonly present. However, the typical triad of disturbed appetite, disturbed bowel function, and early morning waking are not usually clearly marked or are of mild degree.

TREATMENT MODALITIES

Electroconvulsive Therapy vs Pharmacotherapy

There are patients in whom drug use does not yield the expected relief within a period of three to six weeks. In such cases, ECT may prove more effective. Unfortunately, when drugs do not work it is often true that ECT also fails. Even though there appears to be symptomatic improvement with ECT, this may be of short duration. The drug should again be tried in the context of a suitably supportive and reassuring relationship.

ECT may be the treatment of choice when agitation is intense and exhausting, when suicidal urges and attempts suggest the need for rapid restoration to normal, and when there are medical contraindications to drug use or intolerable side effects.

Treatment for Mood-Cyclic Disorders in the Depressive Phase

In the self-limited depressive episodes of the mood-cyclic disorders, the depression mounts in intensity over a period of time (ranging from several weeks to several months) and, having reached its peak, slowly or suddenly subsides. It then may be followed by a manic or hypomanic period, usually shorter in duration. In others, the person remains at his optimal level of function until the next episode—which may occur in a few weeks, a few months, or not until years have passed.

For each person so afflicted, the pattern is usually regularly followed and the frequency and duration of past attacks permit prediction of future attacks with considerable accuracy.

It is in these disorders that amitriptyline may be of particular help in decreasing the duration of the depressive episode and the degree of suffering while it lasts. In most such persons, the drug is as effective as ECT in this respect, and it has the advantage of not interfering with the patient's memory regarding his supportive and sustaining relationship with the doctor. However, it should be kept in mind that with amitriptyline therapy, as also can occur with ECT, patients may experience a shift to the manic phase. As in all disorders, it is the doctor's job to remove obstacles to recovery and to help avoid complications which may lead to future physical or mental pain. For this, a relationship that is undisturbed by amnesia or a sense that a "traumatizing approach" has been used may be preferred. This is usually more easily provided by the use of medication. Long-term results with drug use appear to be better than with ECT, despite the fact that in short-term use ECT usually seems to be more dramatically effective.

Treatment for Depressive Reactions

For depressive reactions and depressive disorders of the psychoneurotic type, psychotherapy is usually the primary treatment. However, medication is helpful in relieving symptoms and in assisting development of the therapeutic relationship. In fact, the medication is especially helpful in treating older depressed patients who may have an aversion toward accepting the fact that psychological problems are basic to their suffering. The medication helps relieve the suffering and enables the patient to cope more effectively with his problems.

DRUG ADMINISTRATION

In all depressive disorders, the patient-doctor relationship is an important reassuring, supportive, and emotionally sustaining factor. In many disorders, it is not the drug alone but also the relationship which meliorates and "cures." It is with the genetically determined disorders that the drug is of basic value in shortening the length and decreasing the severity of the illness. The relationship is a contributing factor in improvement—it is a means of assuring that the proper drug regimen is followed and a means of avoiding complications and removing obstructions to self-healing. In the disorders with fewer biologic changes, the medication contributes to the psychotherapeutic alliance or relationship from which the patient gains knowledge and "strength" to pursue more efficient, pleasurable, and productive social relationships.

Treating the Aged: Special Considerations

When treating older people, the physician must take into consideration that the brain and other organs may have a decreased tolerance to medication.

The need for hospitalization: When depressed patients cannot be relied upon to take medication and do not have family or friends to assist, hospital care may be required. Also, physical illness or the need for support in the activities of daily life or the serious threat of suicide may indicate the need for inpatient care. (Of course, in any depressed patient the possibility of suicide remains until significant remission, so even if hospitalization is not necessary, easy access to large quantities of antidepressants or other drugs should be avoided.)

Discontinuing nonessential medication: Problems can arise when several drugs are used simultaneously, particularly in the aged. Consequently, when possible, nonessential medications should be discontinued before initiating amitriptyline or other drug treatment.

Low dosage: In general, lower doses are recommended for aged patients. A typical dose of 10 mg three times a day with 20 mg at bedtime may be satisfactory in elderly patients who do not tolerate higher doses. However, some functionally able old persons may need higher doses. The debilitated aged, the functionally impaired, or obviously ill do not tolerate the drug as well as healthy old people, but appear to need less of the drug to do equally well. It is as though their illness decreases tolerance but increases drug efficacy.

Discontinuation of Pharmacotherapy

In general, symptomatic and behavioral changes do not mean that the condition or process of the depression has been permanently arrested. Relapse or recurrence is common. This is true whether the treatment has been solely or predominantly psychotherapeutic, pharmacological, or inclusive of environmental change and education.

As the depression lifts, the medicine may be very slowly decreased in amount. It should not be abruptly discontinued (even when all signs and symptoms are gone); rather, the medication should be gradually decreased over a period of time to the lowest amount that will maintain the relief of symptoms. It may be wise to continue maintenance therapy three months or longer to lessen the possibility of relapse. Continued control of symptoms may contribute to psychological well-being and to the acceptance of a helpful, continued patient-doctor relationship. If in the course of maintenance therapy a relapse does occur, the medication may be increased gradually.

Helping the Patient Follow the Treatment Regimen

An old person may be uncooperative and obstructive to treatment, or be cooperative and willing to take medicine as instructed, but forgetful. It is usual for the depressed person to "feel hopeless" and to behave in a relatively noncooperative way "because nothing can help me." There is usually active resistance to continued care and treatment. Simple persuasion to do the family or physician "a favor" often helps.

When memory is poor, some special devices may be helpful, especially to persons who live alone. For example, each dose can be placed in a separate labelled cup. The cups are stacked in order, one on top of the other, with the last for the day on the bottom. This may serve as a reminder of what has been taken, plus what should be taken next.

The "tic-tac-toe board" type schedule with hours and numbers of tablets that should be taken can be affixed to several places: the refrigerator door, the bathroom cabinet mirror, etc.

The physician's prescriptions should instruct the druggist to clearly label the type and dose of medication as well as the times to be taken. The patient should bring all medicine to each office visit so that the patient's perception of the medications can be checked—sometimes a yellow tablet is seen by the patient as olive green, a green as turquoise, and turquoise as blue. Another advantage of having the patient bring medication to office visits is that the doctor can note the number of remaining tablets as a check on proper self-administration.

Paranoid, frightened, or uncooperative patients may fail to take medication regardless of the efforts of family, nurses, or doctor. The physician must try, of course, to permit development of a relationship which inspires confidence and cooperation. It is often helpful to describe a medication as a "tonic" and to enlist the patient's cooperation by pointing out that while drugs do not solve problems, they can and do help individuals to deal with problems more effectively.

Patients' complaints about side effects can often be helpfully dealt with by forewarning the patient and by encouraging him to report them and discuss them freely.

SOME ADVERSE REACTIONS
AND OTHER CAUTIONARY INFORMATION

Anticholinergic Effects

The anticholinergic effect of amitriptyline and other tricyclic drugs may cause urinary retention, including dilation of the urinary tract. In addition, because of this atropine-like action, the drug should be used with caution in those patients with a history of urinary retention.

Another anticholinergic effect which may be particularly bothersome to the elderly is dryness of the mouth. The dryness is usually worse in mouth breathers and with talking. Patients with dentures may complain of looseness in fit and chafing which may develop with the dryness. To diminish dryness of the mouth, patients may be encouraged to avoid mouth breathing and to keep conversation to a minimum. Dryness of the mouth may be misinterpreted as thirst. Rinsing the mouth but drinking only to slake real thirst and chewing or sucking on a slice of lemon or un-sweetened gum (not sweet candies) may be helpful.

Also, vision may be blurred because of the anticholinergic, pupil-dilating effect of the drug. Other possible adverse reactions which may result from this effect are disturbance of accommodation, paralytic ileus, and constipation. In older patients, it is especially important to monitor the bowel condition. Patients may not report bowel inactivity until impaction is present. Paradoxical diarrhea, the release of watery stool around the impacted feces, may be a sign of the condition.

Cardiovascular Effects

Patients with cardiovascular disorders should be watched closely. Tricyclic antidepressants, including amitriptyline, particularly when given in high doses, have been reported to produce arrhythmias, sinus tachycardia, and prolongation of the conduction time. Myocardial infarction and stroke have been reported with drugs of this class. Other cardiovascular effects include hypotension, hypertension, palpitation, and heart block. In addition, amitriptyline is not recommended during the acute recovery phase following myocardial infarction.

CNS Effects

Among the CNS effects which may be caused by the drug are confusional states, disturbed concentration, disorientation, delusions, incoordination, ataxia, tremors, and extrapyramidal symptoms.

Some Other Considerations

Tricyclic antidepressants such as amitriptyline should be used with caution in patients with angle-closure glaucoma or increased intraocular tension. In patients with angle-closure glaucoma, even average doses may precipitate an attack. When amitriptyline is necessary in such patients, the patient or family members should be encouraged to report any changes in vision to the doctor.

Amitriptyline may block the antihypertensive action of guanethidine or similarly acting compounds. Also, caution is advised if patients receive large doses of ethchlorvynol concurrently. Transient delirium has been reported in patients who were treated with 1 gram of ethchlorvynol and 75 to 150 mg of amitriptyline.

SIGNS OF IMPROVEMENT

Criteria for improvement in depressive disorders in the elderly are generally the same as in the young. Signs of improvement in sleep, appetite, and bowel function are usually obvious.

Sleep: The sleep difficulty of depressed people is most commonly characterized by falling asleep promptly and sleeping dreamlessly for a short period with early waking and depressive rumination. In these early morning hours, patients may have suicidal thoughts and even make suicidal attempts. With this type of insomnia, antidepressant drugs are frequently the most useful medications, and hypnotics may not be needed. As the depression lifts, the patient sleeps later. Progressively longer periods of sleep are usually the first sign of improvement and are accompanied by a decreased tendency of the patient to return to bed frequently during the day. Concomitantly, there is a decrease in the patient's longing for night and the opportunity to retire early.

Appetite: The usual pattern with depression is anorexia, although there may be increased eating. As depression lifts, complaints of nausea decrease and food which may have been repellent or repulsive is better tolerated. Patients previously "unable to eat" become able to do so first "because I know I should." Later, they begin to feel a return of interest in food and finally they begin to re-experience hunger. Good appetite returns last. In contrast, for those who have a preoccupation with eating, compulsive overeating decreases as the depression lifts. They then eat in a less driven manner and with more real enjoyment.

Bowel function: With depression, bowel function is usually reduced and constipation may be severe. Spurious diarrhea may occur with fecal impaction. As the depression improves, previous regularity of bowel function is often restored. Amitriptyline may increase the degree of constipation. However, with improvement these effects may subside.

Psychological signs: When a depression is communicated chiefly in terms of subjective complaints, these are commonly worse in the morning and may tend to decrease in intensity as the day continues. The symptoms of subjective sadness, malaise, somatic disturbances, or inertia all may decrease toward the end of the day, and tend to be progressively less intense earlier each day as recovery takes place. Before complete recovery, often only the early morning hours remain difficult.

As depression is relieved, rumination decreases and other psychological complaints usually become less intense. However, depressed patients are often envious of the "healthy people" around them and may express this in a resentful, irritable, querulous fashion. An increase in irritability and querulousness may be indication of improvement. Also, while getting better, the patient may seem worse as he becomes more active and more able to complain.

Improvements in attention and concentration and concomitant capacity to function—which are lost with depression—are usually indications that the depression is moderating. Among these signs are the ability to attend to the conversation of others, to follow radio or television programs, and to read with understanding.

SUMMARY

Amitriptyline may be useful and helpful treatment for all categories of clinically significant depression in the elderly and aged. Generally, it is of primary value in depressions where autonomic nervous system dysfunction is prominent. These symptoms include anorexia or overeating, constipation or intermittent diarrhea, early morning waking, inertia, decreased spontaneity, and decreased concentration. None of these symptoms should be dismissed as "normal for old age" without careful evaluation for the presence of depression.

Usually, the more obvious and severe the depression, the more useful the drug. In mood-cyclic disorders, the drug is important in shortening the length of depressive episodes and in decreasing the intensity of subjective distress. With these disorders, a psychotherapeutic relationship helps keep the patient under treatment and supports him by removing obstacles to self-cure while protecting him from direct or indirect self-harm. Persons with "depressive reactions" and the so-called psychoneurotic depressions can be helped chiefly via reassuring, instructive, supportive relationships. However, these patients may need, and be willing to accept, medicines but have misgivings about psychotherapy. They are amenable to taking a drug to alleviate their complaints and may accept psychotherapy when it has as its vehicle the doctor-patient relationship helped by the medicine.

The aged depressed patient usually has many problems which he is anxious to discuss with the doctor. The antidepressant drug can help prepare the way for a more fruitful conversational relationship between doctor and patient.

AMITRIPTYLINE IN THE MAINTENANCE THERAPY OF DEPRESSION

GERALD L. KLERMAN, M.D.
Professor of Psychiatry
Harvard Medical School
Boston, Massachusetts

Gerald L. Klerman, M.D. is Professor of Psychiatry at Harvard Medical School, Deputy Chief of Psychiatry Service, Massachusetts General Hospital, and Superintendent of the Erich Lindemann Mental Health Center in Boston. He is Chairman of the Advisory Committee on Neuropharmacology for the FDA and a consultant to the National Institute of Mental Health.

Dr. Klerman is also on the editorial board of a number of prestigious psychiatric journals and has been the recipient of numerous honors and awards, including the Lester N. Hofheimer Prize for Research by the American Psychiatric Association in 1969.

He holds membership in a dozen professional societies and collaborated in scores of published research projects on drug therapy of psychiatric disorders.

AMITRIPTYLINE
IN THE
MAINTENANCE THERAPY
OF DEPRESSION

INTRODUCTION

Maintenance therapy of affective disorders has gained increasing attention in the past decade due to a number of factors. Research studies no longer focus exclusively on evaluating treatments for patients with acute episodes, but are increasingly directed toward developing treatment regimens for long-term maintenance of depressed patients' social functioning and lessening the possibility of relapse.

In the middle 1960s, clinical therapeutic studies of the monoamine oxidase (MAO) inhibitors and the tricyclic antidepressants demonstrated the usefulness of these treatments in depressive episodes.[1] These positive clinical experiences led many clinicians to attempt new approaches to the problems of relapse and chronicity. The possible value of maintenance antidepressant drug therapy was suggested for lessening the possibility of relapse and for the further reduction of symptoms as well as for the facilitation of patients' personal satisfactions, family relations, and social adjustment in those patients with chronic depression.

Many of the questions about maintenance therapy have been resolved by recent clinical and research experience. It is now possible to provide a rationale, and to discuss the practical clinical use of maintenance therapy for depressive disorders.

PROGNOSTIC STUDIES

The rationale for maintenance therapy with psychopharmacologic agents depends upon knowledge of the natural history and clinical course of depressive disorders. The basic problem leading to the need for maintenance therapy is that many, though not all, patients experiencing acute depressions for the first time are likely to develop chronic depression or have episodes of relapse. Because not all patients experience these problems, prognostic studies are necessary to provide the clinician with some guides as to cause and outcome and, if possible, predictors of those patients likely to suffer relapse or chronicity. A number of studies that provide the rationale for maintenance therapy have been undertaken in recent years.

The Prognosis for the Acute Depressive Episode

It has long been recognized that the prognosis for acute depressive episodes is generally good. In 1953, Alexander summarized his extensive review of outcome studies made in the 1920s and 1930s, prior to the development of convulsive therapies. He concluded that over 40 percent of hospitalized depressed patients recovered within the first year, and within the second year the recovery rate approached 60 percent. A significant mortality rate occurred due to danger from suicide or from intercurrent infection, malnutrition, or exhaustion, particularly in psychotic depressions of the elderly. These outcomes were for more seriously ill patients with depressions treated in hospital settings.

The advent of the new biological treatments, electroconvulsive therapy (ECT) in the 1940s, and the new "tranquilizers" in the 1950s, served to decrease mortality, to shorten the duration of hospitalization, and to promote the remission of depressed patients' symptoms. In the late 1950s, these encouraging trends were accelerated by the introduction of the MAO inhibitors and the tricyclic antidepressants. By the late 1960s, the outlook had improved further.

Relapse

Theoretically, it is postulated that depressive episodes have their own time cycle and will run their natural course. Modern treatment serves to suppress symptoms while the natural processes of recovery take place. For practical clinical purposes, relapse refers to the return of symptoms within the first 6 to 9 months after the beginning of the initial episode. Symptom-return during this period is considered to be still part of the initial episode, rather than a new episode (a recurrence).

Clinicians and patients should recognize that recovery from the acute episode is seldom smooth. Even with modern treatment, there may be brief periods of return of symptoms, i.e., suicidal ideation, insomnia, feelings of discouragement, etc. These symptom fluctuations occur in up to half of patients after the initial good response to treatment. Their occurrence should not be cause for alarm in either the patient or the therapist. However, skillful therapeutic management is called for.

Recurrence

Recurrence implies that a symptom-free interval of at least 6 to 12 months has occurred. The new episode, the recurrence, represents the emergence of a new phase in the illness. While most patients encounter only a single episode of depression in their lives, a substantial proportion (40 to 50 percent) experience recurrence.[2] Two groups of depressives are of special importance: bipolar and unipolar patients.

111

Bipolar patients: Current terminology uses this designation to refer to patients with two or more affective episodes, one of which is hypomanic or manic. Baastrup,[3] in his study of patients with frequent recurrences, found that bipolar illness recurred on the average of every 8 months in patients in the untreated group. Winokur[2] states that severe bipolar patients treated for mania have only a 14 percent chance of remaining totally well after an episode. Of the remainder, one-half remit from the acute manic episode but have a subsequent episode of mania or depression. The other half remain chronically ill with significant fluctuating depressive symptoms with or without major episodes requiring hospitalization. Although the percentage of depressed patients who are classified as bipolar, or pure manic-depressive, is low (around 10 to 15 percent of all affective illnesses), they are important clinically because of the disruption of family, social, and occupational relationships and the many recurrent episodes in which hospitalization may be required.

Unipolar patients: Patients with only recurrent depressions are more common. Studies by Baastrup,[3] Schou,[4] Angst,[5] and Grof[6] have confirmed the existence of a group of patients who have two or more episodes. With each successive episode, the probability of others increases and the time interval between them decreases.

Chronicity

In addition to patients with a recurrent episodic course, there is an important group that is chronic.

Robins and Guze[7] summarized over 20 follow-up studies of affective disorders, and concluded that a chronic course occurred in 15 percent of the patients. Many other patients labelled "chronic depressive personality" or "depressive character," "hypochondriacal," or "neurasthenic" also have chronic depressions.

PRACTICAL CLINICAL CONSIDERATIONS IN MAINTENANCE THERAPY

The clinician must be able to make practical decisions with regard to selection and management of patients on maintenance therapy.

Goals

In acute episodes, the goals of treatment are the reduction of symptoms of depression and the facilitation of the patient's return to his premorbid state. In long-term therapy the goal usually is prevention of relapse manifested by the patient's social and vocational adaptation, relief from disturbing symptoms, enhancement of personal adjustment, and an increase in the patient's satisfactions with life.

Selection of Patients

The main criteria for the selection of patients are primarily clinical and should be based upon careful review of the patient's history, especially for number and character of episodes.

The following groups seem most suitable for maintenance therapy. They are:

(1) *Patients with chronic depression.* Patients with long duration of depressive, hypochondriacal, neurasthenic, and neurotic symptoms should be reviewed with the possibility in mind that they are candidates for maintenance therapy. Many chronic depressions represent only partial resolutions of acute episodes which occurred months or years in the past. The patients have a partial recovery so that they are not as severely ill as during the

acute episode but may be left with low-grade but continual symptoms of insomnia, anxiety, low self-esteem, pessimism, hypochondriasis, and related symptoms. Often these episodes occur as a consequence of failure to resolve acute grief and bereavement. Even though the symptom pattern may not be that of the classic involutional, psychotic, or endogenous manic-depressive described in textbooks, the presence of significant depressive patterns suggests the need for maintenance therapy.

(2) *Neurotic patients* with a tendency toward chronic fluctuations of depressive symptoms and/or recurrence.

(3) *Schizo-affective patients* with depressive symptomatology. Schizo-affective patients provide difficult problems in diagnosis and management. Very often it is necessary to combine a tricyclic antidepressant with a neuroleptic (such as a phenothiazine, thioxanthine, or butyrophenone).

The value of maintenance therapy does not correlate with the distinctions of psychotic-neurotic or endogenous-reactive disorders. The main criteria are severity and chronicity. The psychotic-neurotic distinction and the endogenous-reactive distinction are only a partial guide to the selection of patients for maintenance therapy. Because a patient has a neurotic or reactive type of depression should not preclude consideration of maintenance therapy.

Dosage

The maintenance therapy dosage of amitriptyline will usually be less than the dose required for the acute episode. The dose will usually be between 50 to 100 mg per day. Since this is a median, there will be some patients who will require higher dosages and others who will require lower dosages. For example, in some patients 40 mg per day is sufficient.

There is great individual variation in tolerance to drugs. Individual dose variation is probably related to differences in absorption, metabolism, binding to proteins, etc. However, after the first months and by the time the patient has entered the maintenance phase of treatment, the medication can usually be administered as a single daily dose at night. Most patients do well with a single ingestion of tricyclics at night during maintenance therapy.

Duration of Treatment

When satisfactory improvement in the acute episode has been obtained, the physician should attempt to reduce the dose level gradually to ascertain the patient's ability to respond to lower doses without return of symptoms. After two months of maintenance treatment with the patient stable, the dosage can be gradually reduced again to see if the patient remains stabilized.

It is not presently possible to predict how long patients should be kept on maintenance therapy for maximal results. However, it is appropriate to continue maintenance therapy three months or longer to reduce the possibility of relapse.

Detection of Relapse and Its Management

Detection: Occasionally patients on maintenance therapy will show signs of relapse. Attention should be given to the patient's characteristic symptom pattern since there tends to be an individual patterned response with the return of symptoms. Typical symptoms to return are: increased ruminations, increase in guilt, insomnia, difficulty concentrating, feelings of pessimism about the future, fall of self-esteem, loss of interest in work, sex, and other activities. When these symptoms occur, clinicians should consider increasing the dose of amitriptyline and seeing the patient more frequently.

Augmentation of treatment: Combined treatment may be necessary depending on the emergence of symptoms. If increased agitation, delusions, and hallucinations occur, indicative of psychotic state, for example, a combination with a phenothiazine or other tranquilizing agent may be indicated. For severe suicidal drive, marked weight loss, or certain kinds of depressive stupor, ECT should be considered.

Hospitalization: Most instances of relapse can be managed on an ambulatory basis by increasing dose and augmentation of treatment by combination with other drugs. Hospitalization may be necessary for patients who have severe suicidal drive, marked weight loss, severe agitation, or inability to maintain their social obligations.

The Role of Psychotherapy

The combination of psychotherapy and amitriptyline treatment is widely used and there are no contraindications to this approach. Drug therapy does not seem to reduce the motivation of patients to participate in psychotherapy or limit the capacity of patients to experience benefit from it. If anything, there is ample evidence that psychotherapy proceeds better with patients who have a marked reduction of symptoms, since too great an intensity of depressive symptoms impairs the patient's ability to derive full benefit from a psychotherapeutic relationship.

Psychotherapy alone will not usually prevent relapse in the depressive patient. One of the very few published controlled studies of the effects of psychotherapy in conjunction with maintenance drug therapy indicated that psychotherapy concurrent with maintenance drug therapy improved overall adjustment, work performance, and communication, and it reduced friction and anxious rumination in a group of 106 anxious neurotic depressed outpatient females.[8] Psychotherapy alone had little effect on preventing relapse or recurrence of symptoms but had a beneficial effect on the social adjustment of the depressed women.

Prescribing Considerations

Systematic inquiry as to the somatic complaints experienced should be made of all patients prior to drug treatment and at regular intervals during treatment. Most depressed patients have symptoms similar to some of those reported by patients on drugs. By carefully inquiring into somatic complaints before initiating drug treatment, these somatic components of the depression can be identified and ruled out to some degree as drug-induced effects. This practice is consistent with that noticed in reports by Busfield, Schneller, and Capra.[9]

Some of the reactions reported with amitriptyline are dry mouth, drowsiness, constipation, palpitations, numbness, tingling and paresthesias of extremities, peripheral neuropathy, and urinary retention.

These and many of the other adverse reactions related to the use of amitriptyline—both during treatment of the acute episode and during maintenance therapy—have been dealt with elsewhere in this text and therefore will not be discussed here. Nevertheless, there are some additional precautions that require consideration when amitriptyline is to be given.

Monoamine oxidase inhibitors (MAOIs): Amitriptyline and MAOIs should not be given concomitantly since severe reactions and deaths have occurred in patients receiving tricyclics and MAOIs together.

If amitriptyline is being used to replace MAOI therapy, it should not be administered until at least 14 days following the discontinuation of the MAOI. Even then, it should be administered cautiously with gradual dosage increases as necessary.

Anticholinergic and sympathomimetic drugs: When amitriptyline is given with any of these agents, including epinephrine combined with local anesthetics, the patient should be supervised closely and the dosage carefully adjusted as required.

Ethchlorvynol: Clinicians have reported transient delirium in patients receiving one gram of this medication along with 75 to 150 mg of amitriptyline. In light of this evidence, caution is advised if patients receive both amitriptyline and large doses of ethchlorvynol.

CNS depressants: It is fairly well known that amitriptyline may enhance the response to alcohol as well as the effects of other CNS depressants such as barbiturates. It may be appropriate, particularly during long-term maintenance, to make the patient aware of this fact and suggest that he be very careful about the amount of alcohol he drinks.

Elective surgery: If a patient is taking amitriptyline and elective surgery is decided upon, it is important for the surgeon to know that the patient is receiving the medication since, whenever possible, it should be discontinued several days before the surgical procedure.

Pregnancy and children: Laboratory data and clinical experience to date are not sufficient to establish the safety of using amitriptyline during pregnancy or lactation. In view of this fact, the physician must weigh the possible benefits of the drug against the possible hazards to the mother and child before giving it to pregnant women, nursing mothers, or women who may become pregnant.

Along the same lines, amitriptyline is not recommended for patients under 12 years of age because of the lack of clinical experience with the drug in children.

CONCLUSIONS

Parallel developments in social psychiatry and in community mental health planning emphasize the feasibility and desirability of the outpatient treatment of depression. In the past, most acute depressions were treated in hospital settings because of the severity of symptoms, the danger of suicide, and the need for medical and anesthesiology services when convulsive therapy was used. However, in the late 1950s and the early 1960s, the usefulness of the new drugs and the growth of the community mental health programs combined to accelerate the ongoing trend toward outpatient treatment.

It is now generally agreed that treatment in the community is desirable because the patient is able to maintain contact with the family, can readily resume or maintain his or her occupational and social roles, can reduce costs, and can be spared the stigma of psychiatric hospitalization. Earlier recognition of depression by physicians and laymen based upon increased sophistication and knowledge, and improved attitudes toward mental illness among the lay public, general physicians, clergy, and school teachers, also have contributed to this trend. Consequently, patients now come into treatment earlier in the course of their depressive illness when their symptoms are milder and more amenable to outpatient treatment.

Maintenance treatment with amitriptyline on an outpatient basis can be considered to be feasible and highly effective. Using relapse rates as the criterion of efficacy, the drug-treated group will experience one-half to one-third the relapse rate of untreated patients.

The selection of patients for maintenance therapy with tricyclic antidepressants in the long-term treatment of depression depends upon the severity of the illness and the patient's clinical history. Maintenance therapy has been shown to be highly effective in preventing relapse in neurotic and psychotic depressives. In conjunction with maintenance tricyclic therapy, psychotherapy can be given to assist the patient with social familial adjustment and to aid in the patient's overall successful adjustment and reintegration into society.

All together, these trends offer hope for improved outcome for chronic depressive patients for whom life without maintenance treatment would be subject to the vagaries of the natural disease course.

REFERENCES

1. Klerman, G.L. and Cole, J.O.: Clinical pharmacology of imipramine and related antidepressant compounds, Pharm. Rev. *17*:101, 1965.

2. Frazier, S., ed.; Winokur, G., Brodie, H.K.H., Klerman, G. and Malitz, S.: Depression and politics, Res. & Staff Phys. *20*:66, 1974.

3. Baastrup, P.C., Poulsen, J.C., Schou, M., Thomsen, K. and Amdisen, A.: Prophylactic lithium: Double blind discontinuation in manic-depressive and recurrent-depressive disorders, Lancet *2*:326, 1970.

4. Schou, M.: Lithium in psychiatric therapy and prophylaxis, J. Psychiat. Res. *6*:67, 1968.

5. Angst, J. and Weis, P.: Periodicity of depressive psychoses. In *Neuro-Psycho-Pharmacology,* ed. H. Brill, Amsterdam, Exerpta Medica Foundation, I.C.S. *129*:703, 1967.

6. Grof, P., Schou, M., Angst, J., Baastrup, P.C. and Weis, P.: Methodological problems of prophylactic trials in recurrent affective disorders, Brit. J. Psychiat. *116*:599, 1970.

7. Robins, E. and Guze, S.B.: Classification of affective disorders: the primary-secondary, the endogenous-reactive, and the neurotic-psychotic concepts. In *Recent Advances in the Psychobiology of the Depressive Illnesses,* ed. T.A. Williams, M.M. Katz and J.A. Shield, Jr., DHEW Publications No. (HMS) 70-9053, Supt. of Documents, U.S. Government Printing Office, Washington, D.C., 1972.

8. Weissman, M.M., Klerman, G.L., Paykel, E.S., Prusoff, B. and Hanson, B.: Treatment effects on the social adjustment of depressed patients, Arch. Gen. Psychiat. *30*:771, 1974.

9. Busfield, B.L., Schneller, P. and Capra, D.: Depressive symptom or side effect? A comparative study of symptoms during pre-treatment and treatment periods of patients on three antidepressant medications, J. Nerv. & Ment. Dis. *134*:339, 1962.

AMITRIPTYLINE/ MAJOR TRANQUILIZERS IN THE MANAGEMENT OF DEPRESSION ACCOMPANIED BY ANXIETY

A.L. NELSON BLODGETT, M.D.
Assistant Professor of Psychiatry
U.C.L.A. School of Medicine
Los Angeles, California

A. L. Nelson Blodgett, M.D. received his post-graduate medical training in psychiatry at Harbor General Hospital in Torrance, California. He is now Head Physician of the Psychiatric Inpatient Ward of the same institution and Assistant Professor of Psychiatry at the U.C.L.A. School of Medicine.

Dr. Blodgett is a member of several professional societies, including the Southern California Psychiatric Society and the American Psychiatric Association.

SCOPE & FOCUS:7

AMITRIPTYLINE/ MAJOR TRANQUILIZERS IN THE MANAGEMENT OF DEPRESSION ACCOMPANIED BY ANXIETY

"There is an old Eastern fable about a traveller in the steppes who is attacked by a furious wild beast. To save himself the traveller gets into a dried-up well; but at the bottom of it, he sees a dragon with its jaws wide-open to devour him. The unhappy man dares not get out for fear of the wild beast, and dares not descend for fear of the dragon, so he catches hold of the branch of a wild plant growing in a crevice of the well. His arms grow tired, and he feels that he must soon perish, death awaiting him on either side, but he still holds on; and then he sees two mice, one black and one white, gnawing through the trunk of the wild plant, as they gradually and evenly make their way round it. The plant must soon give way, break off, and he will fall into the jaws of the dragon. The traveller sees this, and knows that he must inevitably perish; but, while still hanging, he looks around him, and, finding some drops of honey on the leaves of the wild plant, he stretches out his tongue and licks them.

"Thus do I cling to the branch of life, knowing that the dragon of death awaits me, ready to tear me to pieces, and I cannot understand why such tortures have fallen to my lot. I also strive to suck the honey which once comforted me, but it palls on my palate, while the white mouse and the black, day and night, gnaw through the branch to which I cling. I see the dragon too plainly, and the honey is no longer sweet. I see the dragon, from whom there is no escape, and the mice, and I cannot turn my eyes away from them. It is no fable, but a living, undeniable truth, to be understood of all men. The former delusion of happiness in life which hid from me the horror of the dragon, no longer deceives me."

Leo Tolstoi, MY CONFESSION, New York Crowell, 1887.

INTRODUCTION

Anxiety is the most common and the most distressing concomitant of depression, and the chief characteristic of other neuroses. In its milder forms anxiety is a common experience of most of us when we face unfamiliar situations with apprehension. In its severe forms it is so great a discomfort that it demands relief at almost any price. It is the discomfort that arises when the integrity of the personality is threatened and it consists of dread, uneasiness, and tension. The symptoms of anxiety are many and include fearfulness, palpitation, rapid heart rate, sweating, dry mouth, restlessness, sleep disturbance—especially difficulty in getting to sleep—and a vague sense of severe uneasiness. As a response to an external or internal threat it may be adaptive in that it alerts the person to danger and prompts action necessary to correct or forestall the threat. However, the failure to succeed in this may be extremely ego-dystonic and the signal itself may become a danger.

When the experience of depression is examined, the almost universal accompanying occurrence of anxiety can be understood. An essential feature of depression is the withdrawal of cathexis from the outside world and an increasing and often complete focus on the individual's inner world. This focus is always in a punitive, critical, self-deprecating, and derogatory mode. The depressed person ruminates ceaselessly on his past mistakes, sins, and failures. He sees himself as without redeeming worth of any kind. His past is filled with errors of omission and commission; his present is worthless and a result of those errors; and his future is empty and devoid of hope. Escape seems possible only in death, insanity, or physical illness. The price of relief is terrible and unacceptable and inevitably produces anxiety.

The manifestations of anxiety in patients with depressive illness are extremely variable. The range of activity seen may vary from extremes of restlessness and agitation to marked psychomotor retardation and almost complete immobilization. The affect may range from mania and excitement to almost complete flatness. In the excitement and restlessness of the agitated depression, anxiety is very apparent. As the withdrawal of interest and involvement increases, the symptoms of anxiety may be less apparent and more and more difficult to see until the extreme restriction of the focus of consciousness in a desperate search for an elusive answer leaves no energy for anything else. Far from being an evidence of an absence of anxiety, this withdrawn, immobilized state more probably represents the fusion of an extremely high level of anxiety with helplessness, hopelessness, and fear in a final acceptance of inevitable fate.

TREATMENT APPROACHES

While the presence of anxiety may be postulated in most if not all depressive illness, it is not always a *presenting* symptom. When it is the presenting symptom of depression, it is most important that the primary treatment be directed to the underlying depression as well. Unfortunately, this is not always done and all too often one sees restlessness and inability to get to sleep treated by tranquilizers and barbiturate hypnotics which may temporarily relieve the discomfort of the anxiety but may increase the depression rather than treat it.

It has been estimated that anxiety and irritability are evident in about 75 percent of depressed patients. While it is only one of a complex of symptoms, it may often be a troublesome barrier to effective treatment because it produces more subjective discomfort than do most of the others and demands relief more urgently. One of the problems in dealing with depression is the relative ineffectiveness of psychotherapy in providing significant improvement within a useful time span. In a recent study, Klerman et al.[1] found the effects of psychotherapy to be extremely slow. They assessed its effectiveness when used alone as largely restricted to areas of social and interpersonal adjustment. The reasons for this may be clearer when one considers some of the psychoanalytic theories of depression and the depressive character.

Classic psychoanalytic theory sees the depressive character having its basis in a pathologic introject which resulted from the loss of a love object in early infancy. Then, as an adult facing subsequent losses, the depressive character rages at his internalized object rather than the real object of his anger. Thus the ego becomes further impoverished with resulting loss of self-esteem.

Bemporad[2] emphasizes the importance of the dominant other in the depressive's character and the "bargain relationship" which typifies the depressive's mode of interpersonal relationships. The bargain is that the depressive will deny himself autonomous satisfaction in return for nurturance from the dominant one. Bemporad states that the depressive has never learned to achieve satisfaction for himself independently. In the psychotherapeutic relationship the demands for nurturance override any desire for change and the depressive refuses to acknowledge the true goal of treatment. Demands for change by the therapist can be seen as only productive of increased anxiety. Further depression may be the only available defense against that anxiety and the only effective manipulation of the therapist into the desired dominant other. The treatment of most depressive states has therefore come to be primarily psychopharmacologic in the early stages.

PSYCHOPHARMACOLOGICAL THERAPY

Amitriptyline may be a useful drug in the treatment of patients with depression accompanied by anxiety. The gentle sedation of this tricyclic antidepressant often makes it highly effective in helping to relieve mild anxiety in such patients.

In a controlled study, Rickels et al.[3] evaluated the effectiveness of amitriptyline with 108 volunteer subjects with mixed anxiety and depression. All patients were viewed as having either a good or fair prognosis. The evidence of the presence of anxiety was response to questions regarding the three symptoms that bothered them most. On this basis, the group was characterized as follows: 72 percent depression, 42 percent anxiety, 28 percent irritability, 24 percent insomnia, and 18 percent fatigue. Amitriptyline was found to be significantly more effective than placebo in reducing all symptoms. Somatic and anxiety symptoms improved in two weeks and depressive symptoms in four weeks. The relief of anxiety symptoms prior to the relief of depressive symptoms is consistent with the drug's anxiety-reducing sedative effect.

The depressions form a continuum from agitated excited depressions to retarded depressions and encompass a wide variety of symptom complexes. While all depressions have a degree of anxiety associated with them, this is not always a factor in treatment. Where it is, the success of the treatment and the ability of the patient to continue in treatment may depend on the successful management of that anxiety as well as the depression.

AGITATED DEPRESSION

If the patient suffers from an agitated depression he evidences extreme and obvious anxiety as he tries to escape his fears of disaster which he cannot accept. He is ceaselessly active and restless. He paces the floor and cannot sit still. His attention span is very short. He cries, complains, and ruminates aloud. He appeals to anyone and everyone for help. In short, his hopeless fate and helpless state are intolerable and unacceptable. His anxiety level is extremely high and the initial primary focus of treatment must be to relieve that anxiety as soon as possible. In most such cases, his initial management will require hospitalization. He is frequently delusional, hallucinatory, and psychotic. What he asks for is relief of his terrible anxiety and reassurance that all is not lost. What he deserves and needs is recognition of this psychic pain and its relief. This is not to say that the underlying depression should be ignored. It should be treated by a tricyclic antidepressant such as amitriptyline which should be started in therapeutic doses immediately. The initial amitriptyline dose may be from 75 to 100 mg daily. Since the sedative effect of amitriptyline may not be strong enough or rapid enough in action to afford any immediate relief, prompt concurrent treatment with a tranquilizer, such as a phenothiazine, will be necessary in order to help treat the more severe anxiety. The dosage should be adequate to control the anxiety and should be continued as long as it is needed to control the restlessness and agitation. Although the anxiety appears to be controlled, any reduction of the phenothiazine except to relieve adverse effects, before significant improvement of the depression, may only result in recurrence of high levels of anxiety and resulting discomfort. Assessment of the effectiveness of the antidepressant is best achieved by monitoring attention spans, sleep patterns—both early morning awakening and ability to get to sleep—and interest in food. These are much more reliable indicators of effect than the patient's statements. The subjective feelings of relief of depression may be the last symptom of depression to remit. If after one week of therapy there is no improvement in these areas, the dosage of amitriptyline should be gradually increased, noting carefully the clinical response and any evidence of intolerance. If after four weeks of treatment there is no significant improvement in the depression, treatment by electroconvulsive therapy may be needed and should be considered. If electroconvulsive therapy is used it should be remembered that concurrent administration of amitriptyline may increase the hazards of such therapy.

RETARDED DEPRESSION

At the other end of the continuum are the retarded depressions where the most apparent feature is a marked and constant reduction in spontaneous activity. In contrast to the agitated depression, the patient sits still for long periods of time, walks with a stooped and shuffling gait, and shows no animation. He speaks in a monotonous, low voice if at all. He shows no interest in food. His ruminations are secret and not shared. There is little or no evidence of manifest anxiety. In these patients, the treatment is primarily that of the depression, and nonsedating, rapidly acting antidepressants such as protriptyline may be particularly suitable.

In a few patients the lifting of the depression may liberate considerable anxiety and the addition of a phenothiazine may be necessary. This is particularly true when the risk of suicide is high, since the lifting of the depression may liberate the energy to carry out destructive impulses and the resulting anxiety is significant.

THE OTHER DEPRESSIONS

Between these two extremes are a multiplicity of symptom complexes not usually needing hospitalization. It has been estimated that 40 percent of depressions remit spontaneously after following a characteristic course. Usually the onset is acute although gradual onset can occur. The symptoms proliferate and progress up to a maximum, then steadily improve until the episode is over, although attacks may recur. Those that come to treatment often come because of subjective symptoms of anxiety for which they seek relief. This anxiety may be expressed directly as uneasiness, fearfulness, palpitation, insomnia, or frequent crying spells; or it may be observed in restlessness, hand-wringing, rapidity of speech, or sighing respirations. That depression underlies these symptoms of anxiety must be determined by careful history taking and evaluation.

The distinction between depressive neurosis and anxiety neurosis is often very difficult and may sometimes be impossible.[4] A recent study by Prusoff and Klerman,[5] using sophisticated testing and factor analysis, illustrates the great difficulty in making such a differentiation. Their findings indicated that 35 percent of the cases studied could not be successfully classified as either primarily anxious or primarily depressed. Those diagnosed as primarily anxious showed significant depression, and those diagnosed as primarily depressed actually scored higher on anxiety scales than did those that were diagnosed as primarily anxious. Such sophisticated methods are rarely available to therapists, and most must rely on their carefully made clinical diagnoses.

THE USE OF ANTIDEPRESSANT DRUGS

The decision to treat depression with antidepressant drugs must be made with care. Mild depressions which show, primarily, disturbances of mood but without the vegetative, cognitive, or behavioral changes are usually of short duration and rarely require antidepressant drugs unless the characteristic course does not take place and the mood disturbance continues to deteriorate to the point where these changes begin to occur. The decision as to choice of drug when depression accompanied by anxiety requires treatment will depend on the evaluation of a number of factors. The anxiety-reducing sedative effect of amitriptyline will probably be adequate where depressive symptoms of loss of interest in food, constipation, early morning waking, loss of libido, easy fatigability, feelings of inadequacy, and a "blue" mood predominate; and feelings of anxiety are relatively minor and consist mostly of occasional restlessness, infrequent crying spells, and perhaps occasional difficulty in getting to sleep. In this situation, a dosage of 75 mg of amitriptyline should be used initially, and appetite, sleep patterns, and increase in energy and interest should be monitored rather than the patient's expression of relief. This dosage may be adjusted upward gradually if necessary. Usually a dosage of 75 to 150 mg will be sufficient to relieve not only the depression but the milder accompanying symptoms of anxiety. In some cases it may be desirable to give the entire daily dose at bedtime. In general, it is wise to give the patient only small quantities of this or any kind of medication and to see him frequently in order to guard against the ever-present danger of suicide attempt by overdosage.

THE CONCOMITANT USE OF TRANQUILIZER DRUGS

Where anxiety is more manifest and causes more discomfort, in addition to amitriptyline, a tranquilizer will be needed. The choice of tranquilizer is important since these patients are ambulatory and it is important to their recovery that they continue to function as well as possible both on their jobs and in their family circles. The choice generally is between a low dosage of a major tranquilizer of the phenothiazine group or a minor tranquilizer of the benzodiazepine group.

The terms "major tranquilizer" and "minor tranquilizer" are misleading. They do not refer to potency or specific tranquilizing effect but rather to their usefulness in the treatment of major psychoses. The major tranquilizers in adequate doses have a beneficial effect on psychoses and help to control thought disorders, especially those of schizophrenia. The minor tranquilizers have been relatively ineffective in these disorders. The major tranquilizers, however, when used in lower doses than one ordinarily uses in the treatment of psychoses, are highly effective in the treatment of anxiety. When the choice is a major tranquilizer in low dosages, there are three classes of phenothiazines from which to choose:

1. Those having marked sedative effects in therapeutic doses such as chlorpromazine or thioridazine.

2. Those having moderate sedative effect such as perphenazine.

3. Those with little sedative effect such as trifluoperazine or fluphenazine.

When used in combination with amitriptyline, the effect sought is a calming antianxiety effect that does not make the patient drowsy and unable to function. Except in those patients hospitalized with agitated depressions, the first group produces too much drowsiness to be useful, especially in the first week of treatment. Accordingly, drugs in either the second or third group should be used.

In many instances, perphenazine has been shown to be highly effective.[6,7,8,9] The usual dosage used as a tranquilizer for neurotic disorders is from 8 to 16 mg daily. This is significantly lower than the dosage used in the treatment of psychotic disorders where the dosage may range from 32 to 64 mg daily. Nevertheless, phenothiazine side effects must still be considered and occasionally some individuals may have an idiosyncrasy to the drug or be especially sensitive to it. For this reason, the patient should be seen frequently and watched for these possible effects carefully.

When the effect of amitriptyline and concurrent psychotherapy have resulted in a lifting of the underlying depression to the point where a tranquilizer is no longer needed, it can be stopped. While some clinicians prefer the flexibility of prescribing amitriptyline and perphenazine separately, the two drugs have been combined in one tablet (such as TRIAVIL®) which makes administration more convenient. The combined form is available in several tablet strengths which usually provide adequate flexibility and facilitate use.

Although to date there have been no side effects peculiar to the combination of the two drugs, it should be remembered that when perphenazine and amitriptyline are used together the side effects of both drugs are possible. Since the side effects of amitriptyline have been discussed in depth elsewhere in this text, they will not be dealt with here. However, some of the significant considerations related to the use of perphenazine do bear mentioning.

Perphenazine, either alone or in combination with amitriptyline, is contraindicated in depression of the central nervous system from drugs such as barbiturates, alcohol, narcotics, analgesics, or antihistamines. Likewise, it should not be used in the presence of any evidence of bone marrow depression or, of course, in patients known to be hypersensitive to it.

Perphenazine, moreover, has been shown to have an antiemetic effect. This effect has the potential of obscuring the signs of toxicity due to overdosage of other drugs. It may also make disorders such as brain tumors or intestinal obstruction more difficult to diagnose. Since all phenothiazines may potentiate the action of central nervous system depressants and atropine, the dosage of perphenazine should be reduced when the patient is receiving CNS depressants or atropine concomitantly.

One of the most troublesome aspects of therapy with any phenothiazine tranquilizer, including perphenazine, is possible extrapyramidal symptoms—dystonia, dyskinesia, akathisia, ataxia, and the like. Although when these symptoms occur, they can often be controlled by a reduction of dosage or the addition of an effective antiparkinsonian drug, they may persist in some cases even after discontinuation of the phenothiazine. Tardive dyskinesia has also been reported in patients taking phenothiazines. In this case, the symptoms are persistent and in some patients seem to be irreversible. The risk of tardive dyskinesia appears greater with long-term therapy or high-dose therapy, and the condition seems to occur more frequently in elderly patients, especially females. Interestingly enough, tardive dyskinesia may occur after phenothiazine therapy has been discontinued as well as during therapy.

Skin disorders as well as hypertension, hypotension, tachycardia, and EKG abnormalities have also occurred with phenothiazine therapy. A final important consideration is the potential of phenothiazines for causing blood dyscrasias such as pancytopenia, thrombocytopenic purpura, leukopenia, agranulocytosis, or eosinophilia, as well as liver damage such as jaundice or biliary stasis.

REFERENCES

1. Klerman, G.L., Dimascio, A., Weissman, M., Prusoff, B. and Paykel, E.S.: Treatment of depression by drugs and psychotherapy, Am. J. Psychiat. *131*:186, 1974.

2. Bemporad, J.R.: New views on the psychodynamics of the depressive character. In *The World Biennial of Psychiatry and Psychotherapy*, Vol. 1, ed. S. Arieti, New York, Basic Books, 1971, pp. 219-243.

3. Rickels, K., Csanalosi, I., Chung, H.R., Case, W.G., Pereira-Ogan, J.A. and Downing, R.W.: Amitriptyline in anxious-depressed outpatients: A controlled study, Am. J. Psychiat. *131*:25, 1974.

4. Mendels, J., Weinstein, N. and Cochrane, C.: The relationship between depression and anxiety, Arch. Gen. Psychiat. *27*:649, 1972.

5. Prusoff, B. and Klerman, G.L.: Differentiating depressed from anxious neurotic outpatients, Arch. Gen. Psychiat. *30*:302, 1974.

6. Hollister, L.E., Overall, J.E., Shelton, J., Pennington, V., Kimbell, I. and Johnson, M.: Drug therapy of depression, Arch. Gen. Psychiat. *17*:486, 1967.

7. Haider, L.: Amitriptyline and perphenazine in depressive illness: A controlled trial, Brit. J. Psychiat. *113*:195, 1967.

8. Rickels, K., Hutchison, J.C., Weise, C.C., Csanalosi, I., Chung, H.R. and Case, W.G.: Doxepin and amitriptyline-perphenazine in mixed anxious-depressed neurotic outpatients: A collaborative controlled study, Psycho-pharmacologia *23*:305, 1972.

9. Desilverio, R.V., Rickels, K., Weise, C.C., Clark, E.L. and Hutchison, J.: Perphenazine-amitriptyline in neurotic depressed outpatients: A controlled collaborative study, Amer. J. Psychiat. *127*:322, 1970.

AMITRIPTYLINE IN THE MANAGEMENT OF DEPRESSION: AN OVERVIEW

ALLEN J. ENELOW, M.D.
Chairman, Department of Psychological
and Social Medicine
Presbyterian Hospital of Pacific
Medical Center
San Francisco, California

Allen J. Enelow, M.D. is Chairman, Department of Psychological and Social Medicine, Pacific Medical Center, Adjunct Professor of Psychiatry, University of the Pacific, and Director of the Division of Behavioral Science, University of the Pacific School of Dentistry. He is a member of both the Professional Advisory Committee, San Francisco Association for Mental Health and the Board of Trustees of San Francisco Suicide Prevention, Inc.

Dr. Enelow spent fifteen years in private practice and is now or has been a consultant and advisor for editorial boards, corporations, and universities. He holds membership in many professional societies and is a seasoned author/ editor, having published articles, chapters of books, books and monographs, book reviews, videotapes, and films.

AMITRIPTYLINE IN THE MANAGEMENT OF DEPRESSION: AN OVERVIEW

THE DIMENSIONS OF THE PROBLEM

Once when asked to write an essay on the problem of depression in its larger dimensions, I chose the title "The Ubiquity of Depression." This was not just a search for a happy turn of phrase, but represented my growing awareness of the fact that one encounters depression in its many forms every day.

For the practicing physician more than anyone else, depression is truly ubiquitous. Depressed people consult him for a variety of other problems as they perceive them. Some will state that they feel low or depressed; others will complain of fatigue or lack of energy; still others will come with a host of possible somatic symptoms, discomforts, and miseries. Dr. Schwab cites National Institute of Health statistics that indicate that 8 million Americans are depressed. This may be conservative and Schwab proposes that 12 million adults may actually be depressed. Kline's estimate[1] of 20 million depressed adults is also to be reckoned with.

As I've written elsewhere, depression is a basic emotion; it is a psychophysiologic instinctive response to loss or separation, and an important hazard of infancy or childhood. It is a universal response in grief which can occur at any age, but is likely to have important consequences in further emotional development when it occurs early in life. Depression can also be an illness varying

141

in intensity from a moderately incapacitating degree to a severe state that paralyzes thought and action and may require hospitalization. In its many forms, it is a problem that is a large part of the practice of medicine. Depression can create somatic symptoms, it can be a consequence of somatic illness, and it is the most common cause of protracted convalescence.

HISTORICAL PERSPECTIVE AND SOME CURRENT CONCEPTS

In the therapy of depression, Marmor points out that psychiatry seems to have come almost full circle in conceptualizing depressive disorders. From a view of the inherent biological "defect" of genetic origin to a psychodynamic view, we give due credit to the existence of psychodynamic elements but accept relevant genetic and biochemical factors in the depressive reactions. It is clear that the research on central nervous system biochemistry made possible by the tricyclics has given us an insight into these factors that we were not able to achieve previously.

In the 30s and 40s, Marmor points out, certain kinds of depressive reactions responded well to psychotherapy. These were the disorders in which an underlying neurotic personality disorder was a major etiological factor. However, psychotherapy with the more serious psychotic depressions and with the chronic depressions of greater than moderate intensities was almost universally disclaimed. The long-standing chronic depressions in patients who had not known periods of comfort, ease, and feelings of well-being were the most discouraging of all.

Hospitalized depressed patients did seem to respond to ECT. Drugs were primarily mood elevators of a stimulant variety; their effect was evanescent at best. There were reactions when they were discontinued, and they were habituating. In no sense were they true antidepressants. Shock therapy originated in insulin coma research and was followed by Metrazol (pentamethylenetetrazol) therapy. This latter therapy was dreaded by patients.

Since the use of muscle relaxants was not very widespread in the earlier days of ECT, it too was a frightening experience. And very mistakenly, we were immobilizing the patient so that the incidence of fractures was high.

I must say that it was upsetting to do shock treatment at that time and, as Marmor aptly states, the whole concept of ECT still bothers some since we really don't understand its mechanism of action. Also, we have no insight into its effect on brain cells although we have no specific evidence of damage. Nor do we know what it means that some of the patients never recover memory for that period of shock treatment. It may be a retrograde memory defect for periods prior to the onset of ECT. If all else fails, ECT is appropriate. Some feel that the *only* indication for shock treatment is a severe depression of the so-called endogenous or involutional variety where there is no clear-cut precipitant or loss to which the individual is reacting, where the patient has slipped into the depression slowly or had had it for a long time, and where the chemical antidepressants have failed.

Experience with MAO inhibitors and their side effects (which can be dramatic and very difficult to prevent because of the fact that one doesn't have much control over the patient's diet) leads one to conclude that the risks are considerably more difficult to control.

Marmor points out that the tricyclic antidepressants quickly won favor in clinical practice. This is not surprising since psychotherapy and reassurance in conjunction with the administration of tricyclics such as amitriptyline may bring highly effective relief to the patient. Even as the depression is lifting very slowly, there is more of a feeling of hope which can be restored more through the physician's personal influence with the patient than anything else. This makes it easier for the patient to bear that period of time—at least 3 or 4 weeks—before amitriptyline usually begins to reverse the effects of depression. With this approach, patients often report at the end of the first or second week, "You know, I'm feeling more relaxed, even though I'm still feeling depressed." Positive reinforcement at this point by saying something like, "That's good, it shows the medication is working" is appropriate.

Marmor states that the ideal antidepressant, when and if

found, will probably need to be taken only once a day and will manifest its specific therapeutic effects within hours or days, rather than weeks. It will be essentially nontoxic with no significant side effects.

In the meantime, one has to pay a price in terms of side effects and potential toxicity, a price that is worth paying only if the drug is significantly effective and used for the appropriate indications with the appropriate precautions. The tricyclics meet these criteria now.

Marmor proposes that the physician become familiar with the use of the tricyclic agents, and that family practitioners should attempt to treat depression of the appropriate type with tricyclics in everyday practice, rather than referring such patients. Most patients who have not been carefully prepared for it are not willing to accept referrals to psychiatrists. In most instances, either the family physician is going to treat depression or no one will.

The psychotherapy that goes along with administration of any drug for psychiatric indications is something that is, or should be, part of the fabric of medical practice, and does not require the traditional 50-minute hour of the psychiatrist or long periods of time spent listening to the patient without intervention on the part of the physician. On the contrary, as Marmor emphasizes, psychotherapy can be done in relatively brief periods of time and as part of other procedures: taking a history, doing a follow-up visit, during physical examination, in the discussion of findings and recommendations for what should happen, and so forth. Psychotherapy is more an attitude and an attempt to achieve good communication with a patient. At the same time, the physician must communicate the feeling of hope and the feeling that he will do what he can to help the patient feel better. These are really the essential elements of psychotherapy.

The physician may also help the patient a great deal by simple suggestions about increasing social contacts, doing more, etc., and then reinforcing these suggestions on return visits and by approbation if, indeed, these suggestions are being followed. This type of reinforcement helps the patient learn new behaviors, and that is often sufficient. For many people, understanding the psychodynamic basis of the behavior that created difficulties is not really necessary.

Marmor points out with appropriate emphasis that a patient with frequent recurrent depressive reactions developed in the absence of any outstanding life stresses and a strong positive family history provides the suspicion of an endogenous depression. Whether or not this is severe enough to consider consultation is a matter of clinical judgment. A useful generalization is that the general practitioner/nonpsychiatrist physician can treat a patient with the usual doses of antidepressants and if after a reasonable period there has been no response, psychiatric consultation is desirable.

MODES AND SITES OF TRICYCLIC ACTION

Maas, in his discussion of the modes of action of the tricyclic antidepressants on biogenic amine disposition in the CNS, reminds us of the two series of accidental observations made in the 1950s that led to today's use of these agents. First was the discovery that a significant number of patients treated for hypertension with rauwolfia alkaloids developed severe depressions indistinguishable from naturally occurring ones. The second was that patients treated for tuberculosis with iproniazid had elevations of mood. The further discovery that rauwolfia alkaloids produce a depletion of biogenic amines in the brain and other tissues gave the most important clues to the biochemical action of the tricyclics. While their effect appears to be on dopamine, serotonin, and norepinephrine, they differ in their actions. They have in common the tendency to block the uptake of one or more of these amines, thus preventing the principal means of their inactivation. These differential effects appear to relate to their respective molecular configurations.

Maas presents evidence that there may be biochemically identifiable subgroups of depressed patients that respond particularly well to one but not another of the tricyclic antidepressants. This gives us the prospect, at least potentially, of a better classification of types of depression than we now have, and a better utilization of the various tricyclics.

It must be pointed out that we have only suggestive data and that these data do not necessarily tell us as yet *why* tricyclics are usually effective. Nevertheless, it is highly probable that these are the first steps in identifying the mechanism of action.

THE EFFECT OF TRICYCLIC ANTIDEPRESSANTS ON SLEEP PATTERNS

Hartmann's chapter presents one of the most useful explanations of the current state of knowledge about sleep as it relates to depression. He cites research which demonstrates the effects of amitriptyline on sleep patterns in depressed individuals and normals. He points out that sleep has a cyclical nature and that in man there are four or five such cycles each night lasting 90 to 110 minutes each, which involve a regular alternation between *syncronized* (or S) sleep, which is also called "non-REM" sleep, and *desyncronized* (or D) sleep, which is also called "dreaming sleep" or "REM" sleep. S-sleep always precedes D-sleep, and D-time comprises about 100 minutes per night in the young adult. Stages 3 and 4 sleep, or "slow-wave" sleep (the deeper portion of S-sleep), occur almost entirely at the beginning of the night and occupy about 60 to 120 minutes in the young adult.

In depressed patients, there is great variation in sleep patterns with no clear-cut single pattern emerging, except that a decrease in slow-wave sleep(especially Stage 4) is very frequently recorded. Hartmann describes the sleep disturbances of depression: pattern I is characterized as poor sleep, which is reduced sleep time and frequent awakenings during the night with the early morning awakenings and subjective dissatisfaction. This is the most frequently described characteristic sleep pattern of the depressive patient. Pattern II, which is not mentioned as commonly in the literature but which is observed clinically, is the pattern of hypersomnia. Sleep is usually not particularly disturbed, D-time is usually increased, and the D-periods occur early in the night and are long and intense. Hartmann states that persons with mild or neurotic depressions (and especially the young depressives) frequently respond to depression with increased sleep time.

This identification of two separate patterns is an important contribution and one which has not been sufficiently emphasized. These two patterns may exist at different times within the same individual; one of them appears to be an increased requirement for sleep, and for D-sleep especially. Pattern I, however, is not a decreased sleep requirement, but rather an inability to sleep. This may represent extreme agitation or extreme preoccupation with upsetting conflicts and problems rather than a true biological difference between the two. Sometimes patients describe themselves as very depressed, agitated, restless, and upset but at other times during the same episode of depression they feel fatigued, lackadaisical, without mental content, just drifting.

Amitriptyline, as we are all aware, usually has a definite effect on the sleep patterns of depressed patients. Those who are improving on amitriptyline, especially those with pattern I (severely disturbed sleep), show both an improvement in the ability to sleep and an improvement of sleep patterns. That is, sleep becomes more normal in terms of sleep duration and waking patterns as the depression is lifted. The patient reports that his sleep is more satisfying, and this is the first sign of improvement. When a patient reports initial sleep improvement, even with continued depression, the prognosis is good for the antidepressant having an effect upon the depression itself.

In nonlaboratory studies, patients on amitriptyline report that they sleep better and take less time to fall asleep than with a placebo. However, higher doses of amitriptyline produce a less refreshed feeling in the morning. My experience is that a patient who begins on 75 to 100 mg of amitriptyline per day is more likely to report sleep satisfaction than those who receive very high doses of 150 to 200 mg. Although one may choose to give the entire daily dose at bedtime, it is my general feeling that there is a desirable psychotherapeutic effect related to the act of taking a pill three times a day. Patients often report that they feel better immediately after taking a pill, and this is clearly a psychological effect.

Hartmann goes on to describe some laboratory studies in which amitriptyline produces an immediate hypnotic effect and a significant increase in total sleep time and in Stage 2 and Stage 3 sleep time as compared to a placebo. He also found that slow-wave sleep (i.e., Stages 3 and 4) was somewhat but not significantly elevated throughout drug administration. D-time shows a clear decrease, followed by a rebound increase lasting several days upon discontinuation.

Normal subjects have a tendency to feel worse in the morning after amitriptyline, whereas disturbed sleep (pattern I) of the depressed patient improves in all its dimensions, including the subjective effect after amitriptyline. This suggests that, although amitriptyline has a hypnotic effect on nondepressed individuals, it is nonetheless not producing a normal physiological sleep. Still, if the sleep is more satisfying for the depressed individual, the biochemical alterations resulting from amitriptyline use are more in the direction of approximating normal physiological sleep than sleep during the state of depression.

Hartmann concludes that amitriptyline has clear clinical and laboratory demonstrable effects on sleep which are immediate even though we know that clinical improvement with amitriptyline is not immediate. This, of course, may account for sleep improvement prior to improvement in the depression itself.

Continued administration of amitriptyline leads to return of near normal levels for most variables but a continued reduction in D-time. One might speculate that this reflects the fact that D-time (which is usually considered to be synonymous with the time in which dreaming takes place) may reflect unresolved problems and conflicts with which the mind is struggling during sleeping hours at that level of mental functioning possible during sleep. Then when one has helped the individual feel better and resolve these conflicts, D-time will reduce as a reflection of the reduction of unresolved conflicts. Therefore, in this speculative view, amitriptyline will produce improvement both in depression and in sleep-waking problems, making it far more possible for the patient to be amenable to the type of psychotherapy that will reduce conflicts and, consequently, D-time.

Finally, Hartmann concludes that amitriptyline may be especially useful in those depressed patients who have severely disturbed sleep.

DEPRESSION AND PHYSICAL DISEASE

Schwab reemphasizes the fact that physicians and surgeons have the first opportunity to diagnose and treat most of those patients with depression who eventually receive any type of care. It is important to stress the statement "who eventually receive any type of care" because the unfortunate fact is that most patients with depression do *not* receive any kind of care. The economic and social cost to this country of untreated depression must be far greater than can be estimated, because people who are depressed are less productive, less likely to take care of themselves, more likely to become ill, more likely to become involved in accidents, and more likely to be dangerous to themselves and to others.

Schwab's figures mentioned earlier indicate that the prevalence of depression is very great, and he stresses that physicians and surgeons (not psychiatrists) are the doctors who have the first opportunities to offer effective treatment which reduces human suffering and also may be life-saving.

That depression is a "multidimensional sociomedical syndrome" is an interesting concept proposed by Schwab. The five major dimensions are given as (1) *affective distress* (lowered spirits, sadness), (2) *cognitive disorders* (thought distortion, self-disparagement and lowered self-esteem), (3) *psychobiologic disturbances* which are primarily physiological changes due to the alteration in mood, (4) *somatic symptoms* which are the most common presenting features of those depressed individuals who first consult the family doctor, and finally (5) the *philosophic dimension* which appears to be a combination of the affective dimension and the cognitive dimension.

A useful clinical "checklist" for evaluating the depressed patient might include these points: look at his mood, the content of his thinking as expressed to the doctor during communications, his physiological disturbances expressed both in function and in somatic complaints, and his social disturbances as expressed in how he functions in family and occupational roles.

Masked depression can also be called "thinly disguised" depression, since the astute examiner usually can perceive those depressive disorders in which the individual does not speak of his depression, or attempts to disguise his mood disturbance. In fact the so-called smiling depression is characterized by a lack of a convincing smile. But real depression comes through and it is very important that the family doctor learn to become an attentive and sensitive observer.

Schwab discusses the common clinical classification of depression in terms of endogenous vs reactive. In this view, the endogenous type is primarily a biological disturbance, whereas the reactive type is primarily due to a precipitating factor. While Schwab points out that Goodwin and Bunney consider this dichotomy to be misleading, he considers it to have some practical utility for the physician.

Perhaps most depressions are a mixture of biologic and reactive factors with a spectrum or continuum from almost completely biological on one end to almost completely reactive on the other, with most instances being distributed on the continuum at some point other than at the extremes.

This is close to what Marmor discussed in his opening chapter and it is a useful way of conceptualizing it. However, as stated, the distinction between "endogenous" and "reactive" does have clinical utility. As Schwab states, the more "biological" the depression, the more one can put one's confidence in the tricyclic antidepressant drugs; whereas the more "reactive" the depression, the more important it is to stress psychotherapy in conjunction with medication. However, in the case of grief or normal mourning without complications after bereavement, medication should not be used. Nevertheless, many cases of apparently normal mourning after bereavement do become complicated and deepen into clinically significant depression. One must bear in mind that if depression deepens (e.g., three months or so after such a bereavement), then psychotherapeutic efforts should be accompanied by antidepressant therapy.

The classification of "unipolar" vs "bipolar" helps to distinguish the purely depressed individuals from the manic-depressives. But very few manic-depressive patients will be treated by the family doctor in the manic phase. With the advent of lithium and the difficulty in its management, such patients are probably best left to the psychiatric specialist.

In discussing sociodemographic characteristics, Schwab touches on depression in the young adults and the high frequency of depression in adolescence and this deserves emphasis since it is often overlooked. Depression is, of course, as Schwab points out, a common disorder of the elderly. He cites data indicating that higher percentages of elderly individuals than those of other age groups report symptoms that can be attributed to depression. In his discussion of depression in women, Schwab states that it is somewhat more frequent in women in their late 40s and early 50s. The "empty nest syndrome" of women in their early 50s who must change roles because of the departure of their last child is an important medical practice problem because of the frequency with which it manifests itself as a medical complaint. However, social remedies are in order rather than medical remedies. Once again, one must bear in mind that an "empty nest syndrome" may deepen into a complicated depression.

Schwab emphasizes the tendency to overlook depression in black patients, despite the fact that it is being diagnosed more frequently than in the past. Social distance is cited as one of the reasons for this, but perhaps more important is that a significantly smaller number of black patients are at a socioeconomic level where they can afford private care with the type of attention that maximizes the possibility of diagnosing depression. It is the personal concern, interest, and attention of the physician who has sufficient time to pay close attention to the way his patient communicates that makes the diagnosis of depression possible.

Schwab suggests that headache of a low-grade persistent nature is a valuable clue to depression. Similarly, backaches, aches and pains in the extremities, and fatigue are major clues to the possibility of depression.

Depression in low income groups is apparently difficult to distinguish from the manifestations of living under conditions of poverty which in themselves are depressing. However, the patient whose distress comes from social conditions requires social answers and not medical answers.

Schwab has been a strong voice for recognizing the usual relationship of depression to medical and surgical conditions. He has frequently emphasized that depression precedes, accompanies, simulates, or follows such conditions, and it is well to re-emphasize it here. One should never assume that a patient with a physical problem is thereby not likely to have a psychiatric problem too. Medical illness is almost certain to produce some depressive response.

The opposite is also true. All patients who are depressed should be thoroughly evaluated for medical illness, including early malignancies, since depression may be an earlier sign of more serious illnesses.

Schwab states that amitriptyline is a highly effective antidepressant for depressed medical and surgical patients. He cites the kind of complaints in which depression should be suspected, and when diagnosed, suggests that a therapeutic trial with amitriptyline be undertaken. He proposes approximately 75 mg per day in divided doses during the day with the largest dose at bedtime.

With hospitalized adult patients, Schwab recommends gradually increasing doses to a total daily amount of 100 to 200 mg. With outpatients, he recommends smaller amounts, ultimately raising the total amount administered to 100 to 150 mg if necessary. With both hospitalized patients and outpatients of average weight between the ages of 20 and 50, I recommend 75 to 100 mg per day in divided doses with the final dose taken at bedtime. This provides the advantage of the psychotherapeutic effect of the divided daily dose as well as the sedative effect with the bedtime dose. However, objective data validating one approach over the other are not available.

Schwab feels that most depressed patients respond well to amitriptyline, and particularly when the physician utilizes a psychotherapeutic approach. This suggests that the patients should not be given the medication without some kind of supportive therapeutic communication, as well as direct intervention in developing or reinforcing the patient's social support system.

Patients who do not respond well may require an increase in the amount of medication administered or may not be of the group that respond to amitriptyline. Since this group of "nonresponders" is difficult to determine, it is useful to try a tricyclic such as amitriptyline first. Then, if it does not seem to be working after a sufficiently long period of time with doses gradually raised to maximum recommended levels, a trial with another tricyclic or other treatment modalities may be in order.

Some patients, of course, fail to respond to *any* tricyclic. If the tricyclics do *not* work, there are two choices: (1) psychotherapy, or (2) infrequently, ECT. However, there aren't too many patients who fail to respond to some available tricyclic.

Adequate maintenance therapy for three months or longer with gradual reduction in dose is proposed by Schwab. I consider maintenance therapy over a 3- to 9-month period appropriate. The patient can be given the major say in the gradual reduction of dosage by being told that it is time to begin reducing the dose by cutting down by one tablet a day. If no discomfort is recorded after a couple of weeks, a further cut can be made. After a few more weeks, cessation of medication can be attempted. The patient should go off medication at a rate that doesn't frighten him.

Some of the adverse reactions related to amitriptyline are outlined in detail in Schwab's chapter and should be heeded. Moreover, the physician should familiarize himself with the complete prescribing information for this drug before administering.

GERIATRIC DEPRESSION

In Goldfarb's chapter on depression among the elderly, he makes the point that depressive disorders are frequently complicated by physical changes in the chronologically old and aged. Physical impairments include sensory impairment of all kinds, so that there is an interweaving of somatic and psychological factors. Among the conditions that are likely to bring out depression are all progressive chronic diseases. Socioeconomic losses are common as a precipitant to depression and, of course, are most common in the elderly.

Goldfarb differentiates the chronologically old from the "aged" by defining the aged as the old person who evidences a measurable decline of physical or mental functional capacity that interferes with performance of routine tasks. This is a useful differentiation since there is no comparability in degree of vigor and capability in individuals of the same age. Obviously, there are people in their 60s who are physiologically and psychologically younger than some in their 50s.

Organic brain syndrome (OBS) is, of course, of greater prevalence in the aged and may complicate or simulate depression. On the other hand, because depression in the aged can be mistaken for senility, it is important to make the differentiation since depression is usually reversible.

Grigorian[2] has stated that depressed middle-aged and elderly patients are often reacting to a loss and have been unsuccessful in their adaptation to that loss. He proposes that these may be viewed in three different dimensions: (1) qualitative aspects (or what kind of loss the patient has experienced in the past), (2) quantitative aspects (or the actual number of losses that have occurred cumulatively over the years), and (3) the relationship of the present loss to these past losses, and that losses may in fact recapitulate earlier traumatic events that are now more difficult to deal with in the aged person.

Because of the biological changes in this age group, as well as the psychosocial changes, aged patients are often away from their families, away from their old homes or neighborhoods, have lost many old friends, relatives, and neighbors through death and moves to other vicinities, and find their long-established values and beliefs becoming challenged by younger people, as must happen in every generation. Further, the once traditional respect for the elderly is no longer part of our culture, except for some very small subcultures. In addition, most people must live on a much more limited income in their last years. These factors have a devastating effect on the identity of the individual (i.e., how he sees himself as an old man or an old woman). This may be a very much devaluated image of oneself which can be at the core of the depression of the elderly individual.

In all of the depressive disorders, it is clear that the doctor-patient relationship as a reassuring, supportive, and sustaining factor is an important part of treatment approach. In the use of medication with the elderly, one must take into consideration the changes in the brain that may have decreased tolerance to medication. Consequently, it is important to monitor aging individuals more closely than most other patients. And in fact, it may be necessary to hospitalize the patient if he does not have family or friends or others to assist in this monitoring. Nonessential medication should be discontinued before initiating amitriptyline and lower doses of the medication are best used in the interest of safety. A typical dose is 10 mg amitriptyline 3 to 6 times a day.

As the depression lifts, the medication can be slowly decreased in amount and, as with all patients, should not be abruptly discontinued but rather decreased over a period of 2 to 3 months.

Goldfarb makes useful suggestions about how to help forgetful old people remember to take their medication. If recent memory deficit makes it unrealistic for the patient to be responsible for his own medication, perhaps a visiting public health nurse can come once a day to give a single administration of the drug to make sure it is given. There are two problems with the memory deficit of the elderly. One is that they won't take the medicine at all because they forget it. The other problem is that they may take too much because they will forget that they have already taken it. A careful testing for recent memory is an important safety device. If the patient is not suffering from recent memory deficit and there is only the ordinary risk of forgetfulness, it is a good idea to place doses in separately labelled cups, or to use the tic-tac-toe board recommended by Goldfarb.

One should warn the patient of side effects such as dryness of the mouth and blurring of vision. Some additional side effects seen particularly in the elderly include constipation, increased appetite, occasional parkinsonian symptoms, tremor, and hypotensive side effects. In all instances, it is well to recognize that the elderly patient is more physiologically fragile. In addition, the drug should be used with caution in patients with a history of seizures, and close supervision is required when it is given to hyperthyroid patients or those receiving thyroid medication.

The aged depressed patient is anxious to talk with his doctor, as are all depressed patients. The antidepressant drug prepares the way for a more fruitful conversational relationship between doctor and patient, as with all depressed patients. However, the elderly patient may pose a special problem for the busy physician. If such a patient is lonely and wants to communicate with the physician, his needs may be for longer periods of communication than the physician can afford to give. It is important not to turn the patient away, but rather to find means for him to have such communication, e.g., referrals to social workers, social agencies that deal with senior citizens' problems, senior citizens' clubs, etc. Every physician should have at his fingertips one or two social workers and social agencies to whom he can refer patients who need this kind of service.

MAINTENANCE THERAPY

Long-term maintenance therapy is important in order to lessen the possibility of relapse. Clinical experience suggests that the relapse rate from ECT was much higher than it is now that we have the tricyclics for maintenance therapy. The validity of long-term maintenance therapy has been well demonstrated. Since depression usually recurs when medication is discontinued too soon, the long-term therapy should continue for at least 3 months, and in some cases for 9 to 12 months or longer. With maintenance therapy of this duration, the incidence of relapse is very small.

At the point where the patient is feeling comfortable, the job of the therapist is to help the patient restructure his life and to try out some new behaviors both in family and friends that broaden the base of social interaction. The evidence that these things are happening—the patient is doing more, communicating more, being more assertive, expressing himself more, feeling more productive—is the signal that one can begin to lower the dose very gradually. Initially, one dose per day can be dropped, i.e., if the patient is taking 100 mg per day maintenance dose, it may be reduced to 75 mg. If that works well and improvement continues, discontinuing another dose can be attempted. This gradual method can accomplish an eventual withdrawal from the medication and is the best way, in my opinion, to keep the possibility of relapse at a minimum.

DEPRESSION AND COEXISTING ANXIETY

Blodgett defines anxiety as the discomfort that arises when the integrity of the personality is threatened. It is composed of dread, uneasiness, and tension. Its symptoms include fearfulness, palpitation, rapid heart rate, sweating, dry mouth, restlessness, sleep disturbance at times, and a vague sense of uneasiness. While it can be adaptive in alerting the person to danger and in motivating solutions to problems, the failure to succeed in solving problems or reducing dangers may lead to greater anxiety, and eventually the anxiety may itself produce more anxiety.

Anxiety is a very common occurrence accompanying depression, though depression may occur without it. There seem to be depressions that are characterized by anxiety and even agitation, and others which are characterized by retardation and almost complete immobilization. One patient may, in fact, exhibit both types during the course of a given depressive illness. The anxiety also can vary from extreme psychotic restless agitation to anxiety that may only reflect the failure of the depression to lift after a period of time. There are patients who become anxious because they are depressed and simply relieving the depression will take care of the anxiety. There are others who have psychotic agitation or severe anxiety and become depressed. Anxiety related to depression itself may often be reduced as soon as the patient begins to feel the effects of a drug like amitriptyline.

Blodgett states that the depression may be *accompanied* by anxiety or agitation of a significant degree. These patients may require a major tranquilizer in addition to the tricyclic antidepressant. These can be given as separate medications, or in a medication that combines the two.

The phenothiazine is necessary for the treatment of anxiety/agitation, but will not combat the depression when given alone; the tricyclic antidepressant is necessary for that.

At the other end of the continuum of depression are the retarded patients who usually have endogenous or psychotic depression. They sit still for long periods of time, walk with a stooped and shuffling gait, and speak in a monotonous low voice, if at all. They show no interest in food, communicate little, and are characterized by general psychomotor retardation.

These patients do well with tricyclic antidepressants by themselves. The few who do not respond to the tricyclic antidepressants may eventually have to receive ECT.

Treatment must always depend on careful assessment of the degree of depression, the degree of anxiety, and the type of anxiety.

Many of the patients who are agitated, anxious, and depressed will not be able to communicate effectively with the doctor until some effect from medication has been seen. However, the simple act of reassurance and attempting to achieve communication with the patient, no matter how unsuccessful it is in the early stages of treatment, is worthwhile as it sets the stage for more useful communication later when medication has diminished the paralyzing effects of the anxiety and depression.

THE HOSPITALIZED PATIENT

It is in the severely depressed hospitalized patient that one is most likely to find the combination of depression with severe psychotic agitation. An important problem for the psychiatrist, though less so for the general practitioner, is the management of the severely depressed hospitalized patient. There are individuals who feel that ECT is automatically the treatment of choice in the hospitalized severely depressed patient. However, there are others like myself who believe that it is a treatment of last resort, to be used where other treatment has failed.

The treatment of the severely depressed hospital patient is certainly facilitated and made more effective by careful planning of the hospital milieu so that it provides structure, support, a feeling of safety, and containment for possible self-destructive behavior on the part of the patient. However, drug treatment may make such a milieu more effective and I believe in using it routinely unless there are contraindications. If there are no such contraindications, it is useful to begin administration of a tricyclic antidepressant such as amitriptyline as soon as the patient is admitted, in doses of about 100 mg per day. This dosage can be increased to 200 mg as necessary. A small number of severely depressed patients may require as much as 300 mg a day. One dose should be given at bedtime, and if this dosage schedule is carried out so that about 50 mg is given at bedtime, usually no nighttime sedative is necessary.

There are patients, of course, who respond dramatically to hospitalization alone, and this is an example of the use of the hospital environment as a form of crisis intervention. In such instances, one can terminate hospitalization fairly rapidly provided one can be certain that this patient is not suicidal. However, since we know that many patients are most suicidal when they first begin to manifest improvement, it is well not to be too hasty about discharging the patient.

Clinicians agree on an empirical basis that the tricyclic antidepressants may be useful. There are a number of problems connected with the use of tricyclic antidepressants, however. Despite the fact that amitriptyline seems to have its biochemical effect at once, there is a 2- to 4-week delay in reduction of depression, and raising the dose of the drug to heroic levels in early treatment does not help. For this reason, I try to be patient and stick to my schedule in hospitalized patients of average to large body size. With younger and with older patients, I may use lower doses of 30 to 60 mg per day.

In most instances, a patient who has achieved relief of depression in four weeks of hospitalization with tricyclic medication may be safely discharged to outpatient care. A patient who responds in one week is probably not responding to the tricyclic antidepressant and must be watched with caution.

When it has taken the usual 3 to 4 weeks for the depression to lift, frequently patients can be continued on an outpatient basis, where formerly a patient might have been in the hospital for many weeks or months. However, with the advent of the tricyclics, it has been possible to continue treatment and to permit the patient to return to work.

Recently, I saw a patient who was in her late 40s and was having menopausal symptoms who had had a period of depression precipitated by an episode in which she learned of the unfaithfulness of her husband. She became depressed. I saw her on an outpatient basis and within a rather brief period of time she responded, so I did not give her any medication. She seemed to be doing well. I left on vacation, and by the time I returned she had become severely depressed. We hospitalized her because of acute suicidal ideas and agitation. Within three weeks, on amitriptyline and psychotherapy, she was discharged from the hospital. After another two weeks, she was back at work and followed on an outpatient basis.

As with all patients, the hospitalized patient discharged to outpatient care must be followed with a sufficiently long period of maintenance therapy before considering reducing the dose and eventually discontinuing it.

CONCLUSION

It is important that the family physician learn to recognize depression in its many manifestations, some very subtle and some quite obvious. It is important too that the practitioner learn to differentiate depressive illness from normal uncomplicated mourning. The family physician should always bear in mind the complicated cases and the patients whose presenting symptoms are atypical, or whose course does not seem to be what one would expect or predict. Such patients may have depression, and the physician should carefully look at that possibility and attempt to establish such a diagnosis on positive grounds.

Certainly having recognized it, one should learn how to treat it. And the treatment can most often be successfully managed by the general medical practitioner. Supportive psychotherapy is helpful, especially when accompanied by appropriate treatment with a tricyclic antidepressant such as amitriptyline. Where treatment is not successful within a reasonable period of time, one should consider psychiatric consultation.

After successful treatment of the acute phase—whether outpatient or inpatient—continued maintenance therapy is important. Successful treatment may lead to early release from the hospital and continued care on an outpatient basis. In any case, one must be cautious about reducing this dose to minimize the likelihood of relapse.

Finally, the treatment of depression can be a most rewarding experience both for the patient and for the *physician.*

REFERENCES

1. Kline, N.S.: Antidepressant medications, JAMA 227:1158, 1974.
2. Grigorian, H.M.: Aging and depression: The involutional and geriatric patient. In *Depression in Medical Practice*, ed. A.J. Enelow, West Point, Merck Sharp & Dohme, 1970, p. 87.

SUBJECT INDEX

SUBJECT INDEX